THE WOLFHOUND GUIDE
TO

Temple Bar

THE WOLFHOUND GUIDE
TO

Temple Bar

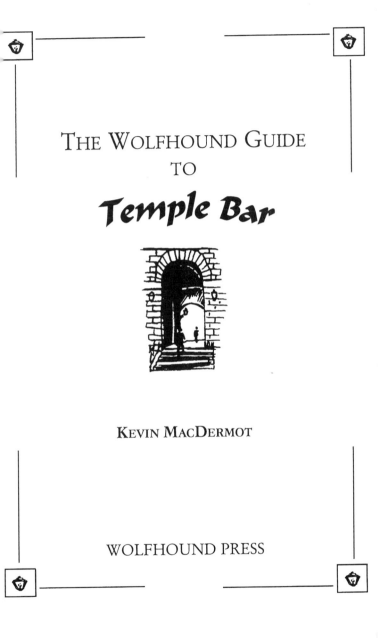

KEVIN MACDERMOT

WOLFHOUND PRESS

Published in 1999 by
Wolfhound Press Ltd
68 Mountjoy Square
Dublin 1, Ireland
Tel: (353-1) 874 0354
Fax: (353-1) 872 0207

British Library Cataloguing in Publication Data
A catalogue record for this book is available from the British Library.

ISBN 0-86327-727-6
10 9 8 7 6 5 4 3 2 1

The author and publishers have made every effort to ensure the accuracy of the
information in this book at the time of going to press. However, they cannot
accept any responsibility for any loss, injury or inconvenience resulting from the
use of information contained in this guide.

Photographs: Jan de Fouw
Line Drawings and Map: Ann Fallon
Cover Illustration: Nicola Emoe
Cover Design: Slick Fish Design, Dublin
Typesetting: Wolfhound Press
Printed by Edelvives, Spain

Contents

Acknowledgements

Thanks to Jenna for her help in compiling this book and keeping me company on the many footslogs around Temple Bar.

Thanks to Emer, Dave and all at Wolfhound for their help and patience in putting together a guide which required more work and time than any of us could have imagined. Thanks to Maria who came up with the idea in the first place.

Thanks to Temple Bar Properties for their help and assistance, and access to all of their own publications and records, without which this book could not have been completed.

A special note of thanks to author Pat Liddy whose historical work *Temple Bar — Dublin*, published by Temple Bar Properties, was an invaluable guide to the history of the area.

Introduction

Temple Bar is rooted firmly in Irish history. Until the dissolution of the monasteries in 1537, the land in this area was owned by the Augustinian Order. Rather than recognising its links with the Augustinians, however, Temple Bar takes its name from Sir William Temple who bought the land in the latter part of the sixteenth century. This English-born aristocrat arrived in Ireland in 1599, and in 1609 was elected Provost of Trinity College. The college is located beside the area where he built his home and gardens. It is interesting to note that the first known appearance of Temple Bar on a map of the city of Dublin was in 1673.

The more ancient history of the area still lives on in the names of some of the bars and streets of Temple Bar. The Norseman pub, and the Isolde's Tower bar recall the city's Viking heritage, while a number of the streets still accurately trace the perimeter of the old city's walled fortifications. The first recorded Viking raid on Ireland came in 795, but in 837 a Viking fleet of around sixty ships sailed into the Liffey. Four years later, the Vikings returned to build a well-defended port which evolved into the merchant port of Dyflin. Dyflin did not become a permanent fixture until the ninth century when

Dublin's Vikings eventually began to build a fortified town on high ground near the port.

Even after the defeat of the Vikings by the King of Munster, Brain Ború, in the famed battle of Clontarf in 1014, the Norse king, Sitric IV, was allowed to remain in Dyflin. Although the power of the Vikings had been broken, they stayed on, intermarried with the Irish, and forged a Hiberno-Norman identity for the city. This ended in 1170 when the Anglo-Normans, led by Strongbow (Richard de Clare), and invited to Ireland by Diarmaid MacMurchada, defeated them in battle. The Hiberno-Normans moved across the river into the area known as Oxmantown, where they eventually were subsumed into the general population.

Sea-power had been the key to the piracy and strength of the Vikings, and Dublin, with its natural harbours, was an ideal location to found a city. Their oak 'dragon ships' could raid inland Irish and British waterways at will, although Viking fleets of more than a hundred ships raided as far south as Tangiers and Constantinople.

The importance of the river to Dublin has always been very clear. The city's name in Irish, Baile Átha Cliath, means 'The Town of the Hurdle Ford', and derives from an old river crossing which is still identifiable.

Today the link with its Viking past is very much in evidence in Dublin. The Dublin Viking Adventure centre, which is near Christchurch Cathedral, celebrates the link with the Norsemen. The Dublinia exhibition at Christchurch Cathedral also celebrates the city's history — albeit a slightly later one — describing itself as a 'bridge to the medieval past'.

Medieval Dublin centred around the Dubh Linn (the black pool), which gave the city its present-day name. As it began to expand westwards, it suffered a number of setbacks, beginning with an attempted Scottish invasion in 1316, and followed by the devastation wrought by the Black Death in 1348.

A revolt led by Silken Thomas Fitzgerald in 1534 ended in failure and a humiliating end for the young pretender (he became a servant of the English monarchy), while the monasteries were dissolved in 1537, under Henry VIII's rule.

With the defeat, by William of Orange, of the English Catholic king, James II, at the Battle of the Boyne in 1690, came the harsh anti-Catholic penal laws, the rise of the Protestant Ascendancy, and boom times for the capital city. The eighteenth century saw Dublin become the second largest city in the British Empire, and the fifth largest in Europe, and it was in the seventeenth and eighteenth centuries that Temple Bar began to expand as its proximity to the river gave it added importance.

After the dissolution of the monasteries, the area was given the name Temple Bar, the latter word referring to a riverside walkway. Much of the marshy ground had been reclaimed from the river, but as development in the area continued apace, the bog disappeared, to be replaced by quays and streets.

During the seventeenth and eighteenth centuries Temple Bar gained something of an unsavoury reputation as a focal point of attraction for the lower elements of Dublin society. It was known as a centre for crime and prostitution, pubs and rebels. However, during the 1800s, the area began to change its image, and transformed itself into a bustling centre for the small traders, craftsmen and businesses of the city.

Though Temple Bar now has something of a Bohemian reputation, this was not always the case, and it was only in recent years that the area was saved from the wrecker's ball. Large swathes of the area were owned by CIÉ (the state transport company), which planned to clear much of it to accommodate a new central bus terminal on the south side of the Liffey, right in the heart of the city. Development of the site and the idea was slow, and in the meantime the properties owned by CIÉ were let on short-term leases at low rents.

The area began to thrive and the bus terminus idea was abandoned in the 1980s when a decision was taken to develop Temple Bar as a centre of entertainment, shops and culture. That plan was given a tremendous boost in 1991 when Ireland became the Culture Capital of Europe, and plans to turn the area into a cultural quarter were rapidly accelerated.

The Temple Bar area is now better than ever, with tourists mingling with locals, people out for a quiet meal in a good restaurant, strolling through streets packed with young people out on the town. The area has led Dublin and Ireland's charge

into the 1990s, persuading many that the city is worth sticking around in, rather than take the traditional route of emigration. Business people in the area are confident that Temple Bar will maintain its reputation as a centre for good food, art, culture and entertainment.

The cafés, shops and eateries that constantly spring up in Temple Bar are proof that the area is continuing to evolve, as its reputation begins to spread. With hundreds of restaurants, pubs, clubs, galleries and theatres, Temple Bar remains the cultural heart of Dublin, successfully linking the city's history with its modern needs.

TEMPLE BAR PROPERTIES

Eustace Street
Temple Bar
Dublin 2
Tel. (+353 1) 677 2255

Temple Bar Properties (TBA) was set up under the Temple Bar Area Renewal and Development Act, 1991, to oversee the area's transformation into Dublin's 'cultural quarter'. Its mandate extended beyond the development of a cultural quarter, part of its remit being to establish a residential and small-business community to ensure the continued presence of visitors in the area. Today the responsibility for overseeing the continuing development of the area is shared by Temple Bar

Properties and Temple Bar Renewal Ltd, a state company. Both are also responsible for providing visitors and locals with information on the area.

It is difficult to picture the Temple Bar area as it was just over a decade ago — dominated by buildings in a state of either disrepair or dereliction. TBA is responsible for the area's rejuvenation. The main objective of the scheme was to encourage investment by the private sector in areas which would otherwise have been ignored by speculators. This was achieved by offering a variety of tax incentives, including tax relief for owner occupiers of certain residential premises, capital allowances on the expense of refurbishing factories, and double rent allowance for traders leasing new or refurbished premises.

Today the company's cultural policy is to work with artists, organisations and anyone interested in maximising the area's cultural potential. Future Projects for TBA include the setting up of a photographic archive of the National Library of Ireland and the erection of a new home for the Project Arts Centre.

Map of Temple Bar

Information

GETTING THERE

By Air

Dublin Airport has a tourist office and a bureau de change. Buses leave regularly for town from outside the departures exit, while Airlink buses will take you to the central bus station, known as Busáras. Buy your ticket onboard. The Airlink will cost around £2.50, but you could get the normal service, No. 41 bus, which will drop you off in the city centre, and at £1.20 is cheaper. Temple Bar is only a short walk across O'Connell Bridge from the bus stop. A taxi from the airport will cost you around £12.

By Ferry

If you land at Dublin Port you'll need to get bus No. 53 to the city centre. From Dún Laoghaire, the quickest route to town is via the DART (Dublin Area Rapid Transit, the local train service), which you'll find right outside the ferry port. The DART will cost you around £1 to get into town, and takes only about 20 minutes.

Information

ARTS AND CULTURE

As a city, Dublin is justifiably proud of its literary heritage, and can claim many famous authors and playwrights. Though it is still for these that the city holds its reputation as a centre of culture, Temple Bar is helping to promote the visual arts by housing a large number of new artists, sculptors and crafts-people. However, if you do need a literary companion to help you along your way, you could do worse than to choose from the works of James Joyce, Jonathan Swift, W.B. Yeats, Brendan Behan, Oscar Wilde, George Bernard Shaw or even Bram Stoker.

BEHAVIOUR

Like the people of the city, Temple Bar is easy going — shorts and a T-shirt are as acceptable here as a suit and tie. Though you may feel inclined to dress smartly for some of the more exclusive restaurants, in the main, jeans can be worn anywhere. Perhaps the only people who are really likely to question your manner of dress are the bouncers on duty at the quarter's night-clubs. Unfortunately there's no hard and fast rule to get you past this breed of native, and it very often appears that many of them make up the rules as they go along.

There are few rules, other than the law, that you have to worry about breaking, although you should be advised that conversations regarding politics and religion can often become heated, especially in the bars!

BUSES

Dublin has a regular, if somewhat grimy, bus service. Travelling around the city will generally cost you about £1 per journey. You can pay the driver directly, or you can buy a card of tickets, which works out slightly cheaper. More information is available from Dublin Bus — tel. (+353 1) 873 4222.

CLIMATE

The best advice when getting ready for a day out in Temple Bar is to prepare yourself for all eventualities. The Irish weather is nothing if not unpredictable so you shouldn't take a blast of sun at 8 a.m. as a guarantee that it will still be there at noon.

Average temperatures in Dublin in the summer hover somewhere between 15 and 20 degrees centigrade, while in winter they fall to between 4 and 8 degrees centigrade.

Although there's a lot of rain, the weather usually doesn't reach freezing conditions, mainly because of the influence of the Gulf Stream. In the winter there isn't much snow, and it rarely settles in the city for very long, but in the summer it is possible to encounter heatwaves.

During the summer months, there are around 18 hours of sunlight, and it remains light until after 11 p.m. In winter, darkness can fall as early as 3 p.m.

DENTAL

Emergency dental care is available at the Dublin Dental Hospital, at the rear of Trinity College — tel. (+353 1) 612 7391.

DISABLED TRAVELLERS

Things are improving greatly in Ireland for disabled travellers, as more and more guesthouses and hotels become adapted for special needs. Bord Fáilte's Accommodation Guide gives a good break-down of which places are suitable for wheelchairs, or you could contact the National Rehabilitation Board — tel. (+353 1) 668 4181.

ELECTRICITY

Electricity is 220 V, 50 Hz.

Adaptors for plugs: you'll need the flat three-pinned variety, which can be purchased at any electrical or hardware store.

EMERGENCIES

Gardaí/Police

The Gardaí — Irish police — are very courteous to tourists, so don't be afraid to ask them for help of any kind. In case of emergency, dial 999 on the nearest telephone, and say whether you're reporting a fire, police or medical problem. Then you'll be asked for your location.

If you are mugged or robbed, report the crime. If you have your passport or money stolen, contact the Tourist Victim Support network by asking the Gardaí for a referral. They'll help you to contact your embassy/bank.

Tourist Victim Support — tel. (+353 1) 478 5295

Victim Support — tel. 1800 661 771

Rape Crisis Centre — tel. (+353 1) 661 4911

The Samaritans — tel. (+353 1) 872 7700

Drug Advisory and Treatment Centre — tel. (+353 1) 677 1122

FAX

Faxes can be sent from any shops that provide stationery or photocopying services.

GAY/LESBIAN DUBLIN

Though the gay scene in Dublin is still quite small, it is growing. There are several pubs and clubs that are gay, and there are many others that are gay-friendly.

The best way to catch up on the gay scene is by getting a copy of the *Gay Community News*, the freesheet which you can pick up in many city-centre locations. There are also a number of gay/lesbian organisations in Dublin.

Dublin Lesbian Line — tel. (+353 1) 872 9911

Gay Switchboard Dublin — tel. (+353 1) 872 1055

LOT (Lesbians Organising Together) — tel. (+353 1) 872 7770

LEA (Lesbian Education and Awareness)
    — tel. (+353 1) 872 0460

Outhouse (Gay and Lesbian Community and Resource Centre
    — tel. (+353 1) 670 6377

HEALTH

For immediate needs, you should phone the emergency services on 999. Your hotel should be able to provide you with a list of the nearest local services.

There are several chemists and pharmacies around the area who will be able to supply you with the usual everyday medical supplies, although a written prescription from a doctor will be necessary when requesting more restricted medicines.

LANGUAGE

English is the main language although the native Irish language is making a bit of a comeback. The Dublin brogue can be hard to make out at times, but few people will be offended if you ask them to repeat themselves as they'll probably be too busy trying to figure out what you just asked them!

MONEY

Though the Euro will become much more important in the coming years, the Irish pound — or the punt — remains the basic form of currency. The Irish pound is divided into 100 pennies, and there are 1p, 2p, 5p, 10p, 20p, 50p and £1 coins, as well as £5, £10, £20 and £50 notes. There are larger notes available, but it's not always a good idea to be seen using large notes.

Changing money is fairly straightforward although you should expect to be charged a commission for such services.

Shops and pubs won't expect to be given the exact amount for a purchase, but other organisations will. Buses are the most notorious, so make sure you have the right amount of money for your fare.

Information

NEWSPAPERS

There are three main Irish broadsheet newspapers, one Dublin evening newspaper and a number of mainly English-inspired tabloids.

Of the broadsheets, the *Irish Independent* has the best news coverage but is let down by its rougher image, while *The Irish Times* is the solid paper of record. *The Examiner* is the third broadsheet and is striving to break the grip on the national scene held by the other two papers, an aim which it seems to be achieving.

For regular listings in Dublin, the *Evening Herald* is quite useful. It also gives the day's sports and news, albeit in true tabloid style.

There's also a freesheet, which is widely available throughout the city centre, and particularly in Temple Bar — the *Events Guide* gives a complete listing of what's on where, as well as containing a few good articles.

OLDER TRAVELLERS

Senior citizens are entitled to a wide number of discounts and free entry to travel and tourist facilities, although in most cases you will have to provide proof of age, or have a pass. The age to qualify for such discounts in Ireland is normally between 55 and 60 years of age for women, and between 60 and 65 years of age for men.

OPENING HOURS

Banks: Mon to Fri: 10 a.m. to 4 p.m. There are also numerous 24-hour ATMs (Automatic Telling Machines) dotted around the city, which will let you withdraw money from visa and other credit card accounts. Be careful when using such machines, especially at night, as muggers watch for tourists, and locals, using cash-points.

Business Hours: 9 a.m. to 5 p.m.

Pubs: winter opening hours are from 10.30 a.m. to 11 p.m., while summer opening hours are from 10.30 a.m. to 11.30 p.m. Some bars also have special late licences which allow them to remain open until around 1 a.m. At the moment, the debate is raging between vintners and politicians on the subject of extending the opening hours for bars, but no deal has been reached as yet.

Restaurants: Lunch — 12 noon to 2.30 p.m.

Dinner — 5.30 p.m. to 11 p.m. Cafés stay open all day.

Shops: Mon to Sat: 9 a.m/9.30 a.m. to 6 p.m., although some of the larger supermarkets have extended shopping hours. There are also numerous mini-centres (try Spar on Parliament Street), which are open until late at night. And there's an all-night shop on Dame Street. Late-night shopping is on Thursday night, when most shops stay open until 8 p.m. Sunday opening is restricted, but some shops do trade.

POPULATION

There are around 5 million people on the island of Ireland, and upwards of 500,000 of these live in Dublin city, while another 1.5 million live within commuting distance. Although the country has some of the best services for pensioners, it's the younger segment of the population that has given Ireland its popular image as a young, vibrant place to live.

POST

You can post letters and postcards in any of the numerous green post-boxes dotted around the city. The boxes are regularly emptied during the day. Stamps can be obtained at any post office, and some newsagents are also licensed to sell them.

RADIO AND TELEVISION

The state broadcasting company is Radio Telefís Éireann, known as RTÉ; it controls two television channels and a number of radio stations. There are also two other Irish television channels — TV3 and the Irish-language TnaG.

In Dublin you'll have access to a wide number of satellite channels, including Britain's BBC, ITV and Channel 4, Sky News and Sports and CBS services, together with the French TV5.

On the radio there are numerous independent stations, of which FM 104, 98FM and Today FM are the most popular in Dublin.

TAXI

Taxis in Dublin are expensive, with a call-out charge of around £1.80. There is also a charge of about 40p per extra passenger or piece of luggage, and a similar charge for late-night runs, from 8 p.m. to 8 a.m.

Generally, you can hail a taxi in the street, or go to one of the taxi-ranks dotted around the centre of the city. But be warned — taxis are as rare as leprechauns in early-morning Dublin when the pubs and clubs empty.

If you have any complaints about taxis, call the Garda Carriage Office — tel. (+353 1) 873 2222.

TELEPHONE

There are many public phones around the area, though you will find that most public phones now use phonecards rather than coins. These can be obtained from any post office and most newsagents. They are sold in units, ranging in size from 10 to 50 units.

Pubs often have pay-phones for customers' use, but you

Information

can expect to pay between 50 and 100 per cent more for use of these phones.

If you need to find a number, you can either use the telephone directory or call directory enquiries on 1190 for local numbers, 1197 for cross-channel (British) numbers or 1198 for international numbers. This service is free from public payphones.

TIPPING

Though most restaurants will include a service charge (around 10 per cent) for large parties, they don't add it on for smaller groups, so tipping is usual. Few people tip in bars and cafés, but almost everyone does in restaurants and hotels. Usually a tip of 10 per cent is given at the counter or left on the table.

TOILETS

Although there are some public toilets around the area, most people use those in bars, restaurants and hotels. Women's toilets are usually denoted by the Irish word MNÁ, while men's toilets are marked FIR.

TOURIST OFFICES

First port of call should be the Temple Bar Information Centre which has details of what's on in the area. This can be found at 18 Eustace Street — tel. (+353 1) 671 5717.

The head office of the tourist board, Bord Fáilte, is at Baggot Street Bridge — tel. (+353 1) 676 5871/ 602 4000 — but the tourist office at St Andrew's Church in Suffolk Street, near Trinity College, is much more accessible.

The tourist board will provide information on the city and the country, and will book accommodation for you, for a small fee. The computerised information and reservation service is known as Gulliver, and contains information on most things you'll need to know — tel. 1 800 600 800.

Information

TRAFFIC

Though traffic in Dublin can be a frustrating and unnerving experience at the best of times, Temple Bar rarely suffers from such problems, being a mainly pedestrian area. If you do venture outside the quarter though, be aware that traffic is fast-moving along most roads bordering Temple Bar. There are many pedestrian crossings situated at traffic lights, where a green man (electronically displayed) will signal that it's safe to cross. Most of the pedestrian crossings also have an aural beeping and/or voice command, to tell anyone with sight difficulties when it's safe to cross.

CALENDAR

BANK/PUBLIC HOLIDAYS

New Year's Day, 1 January

St Patrick's Day, 17 March

Good Friday

Easter Monday

May Day Holiday, 1 May

June Holiday, 1 June

August Holiday, 1 August

October Holiday, last Monday in October

Christmas Day

St Stephen's Day

(St Patrick's Day, Christmas Day, St Stephen's Day and May Day holidays are taken on the following Monday, if they fall at a weekend.)

CULTURAL AND SPORTING

March: International Film Festival.

Six Nations (formerly Five Nations) rugby competition starts, featuring matches against England, France, Scotland Wales, and now Italy.

St Patrick's Day, which now attracts more than 500,000 people onto the streets of Dublin, complete with marching bands and Mardi Gras atmosphere.

April: The Easter Rising of 1916 is commemorated during Easter week.

On 13 April excerpts of Handel's Messiah are performed at the site of the former Music Hall on Fishamble Street.

May: The Digital Film festival begins in Temple Bar towards the end of the month.

RTÉ Proms. RTÉ's and the National Symphony Orchestra combine at the Royal Dublin Society in Ballsbridge.

June: Bloomsday on 16 June sees Dubliners retrace the steps of Leopold Bloom, James Joyce's famous character in *Ulysses*, holding readings and drinking pints of stout and porter along the way, while all the time dressed in period costume.

Festival of Music in Great Irish Houses. Classical concerts take place at some of the many grand and stately homes across the country, including a number in the Dublin area.

July: The James Joyce Summer School begins at Newman House, St Stephen's Green, and the James Joyce Centre, North Great George's Street — lectures, seminars and social events.

Temple Bar Blue Grass Festival kicks off in the city's cultural quarter, involving a vast array of gigs in the area's bars and pubs, as well as endless conversations, films and workshops on the subject matter.

August: The Dublin Horse Show is held at the Royal Dublin Showground. Although the show revolves around equine pursuits, it's also famous for giving the city and country's social élite the chance to show themselves off.

September: The All-Ireland football and hurling finals take place at the Gaelic Athletic Association's headquarters in Croke Park.

The Dublin Theatre Festival begins and runs for over two weeks.

October: The Oscar Wilde Autumn School begins, focusing on the life, works and times of the great author and playwright.

The month ends with the running of the Dublin Marathon

Part One

Street Guide

ADAIR LANE

Dating from around 1840, this street was named after Sir Robert Adair who owned property in the area. It was originally built to provide access to stables owned by the grand houses of Aston Place and Price's Lane.

ANGLESEA STREET

One of the oldest and best-known streets in Temple Bar, Anglesea Street has existed since around 1658, but has been redeveloped continuously over the centuries. Named after the First Earl of Anglesea, Arthur Annesley who owned extensive property and houses in the area near College Green, the street has been home to milliners, coachmakers and tailors; it is now lined with modern restaurants and pubs. The Annesley name has also survived in greater Dublin, and sight-seers will encounter a number of areas named after the original Earl.

Stock Exchange

Temple Bar may seem an unlikely setting for trading, but the Dublin Stock Exchange can be found at 5 Anglesea Street, where it has been since the 1870s. The Victorian interior of the Exchange has survived through the intervening years, although these days it has to compete for attention with the technology of modern financial wheeling and dealing.

ASDILL'S ROW

Originally laid out around 1820 as a tenement area, this street was named after John Asdill, a local merchant with connections to the Russian Empire. Asdill's Row is unique in Temple Bar in that the Crampton Building flats, built in 1890 by the Dublin Artisans' Dwelling Company, still serve a local, long-standing community, which has survived in spite of the changes to the area.

ASTON QUAY
& ASTON PLACE

Laid down in the first half of the 1700s, both Aston Quay and Aston Place are believed to take their names from the merchant Henry Aston, who rented this land around 1672. It was under Aston's supervision that a part of the river Liffey was reclaimed and enclosed to make a quay. Now a prime business location, this area was one of the poorest in the city in the 1700s, but still numbered ironmongers, cobblers and glass-menders among its businesses.

Aston Place achieved deserved fame at the start of the 1900s through its excellent second-hand bookshops. Ironically, however, just as Temple Bar was about to enter its greatest period of housing art and crafts in the 1990s, the last link to this literary heritage was lost when the Three Candles Print building was sold in 1991 to the Union of Students in Ireland.

Virgin Megastore

Originally the home of McBirney, Collis & Co. (Silk Merchants and Drapers), this beautiful and impressive building has retained its link with retailing down to the present day, and is currently owned by the Virgin Group. However, evidence of the store's former owners can still be spotted above the entrance.

BEDFORD LANE
& BEDFORD ROW

Named after the Fourth Duke of Bedford and Lord Lieutenant of Ireland 1757–1761, John Russell, both these narrow passageways still primarily serve the same function for which they were laid down in the 1760s — that of access.

Bedford Row, however, has more of a claim to interest than its namesake. The row was home to a 'fancy painter' in the eighteenth century. More recently, it featured in James Joyce's literary masterpiece, *Ulysses*, when the celebrated Stephen Dedalus searches through the books of Clohissy's Bookshop — which once stood at numbers 10 and 11 — for a pawned school prize.

CECILIA STREET

Still dominated by **Cecilia House**, some mistakenly believe this street to have been named for St Cecilia, the patron saint

of music. In fact, it was named after Cecilia Fownes, one of the Fownes family responsible for much of the early development of the area. Until the 1760s it was part of Crow Street.

Cecilia House was built on the site of a medieval Augustinian friary — a centre of worship of the order, which owned much of the surrounding lands until the dissolution of the monasteries in 1537. The building has entertained a variety of owners and guests; at different points in its history, it has been home to the once renowned Crow Street Theatre, and to the Catholic University School of Medicine.

Crow Street Theatre

Built around 1760 on the site of the old Dublin Academy of Music, the Crow Street Theatre played host to impressive audiences of 2,000 people, and for a while enjoyed an international reputation for its performances. Unfortunately, Crow Street Theatre fell foul of the same violence and dipping fortunes that saw the eventual closure of numerous city rivals. Under the new name of the Theatre Royal, it was beset by a rising number of audience riots and falling receipts; its curtain fell for the last time in 1820.

COLLEGE GREEN

One of the most famous parts of Temple Bar, College Green takes its names, as one might expect, from Trinity College, which was founded in 1592. The green was formerly known as Hoggen Green, after the convent of St Mary de Hogge, which had stood in the area since the twelfth century.

Trinity College itself stands on the ground where the Augustinian monastery of All Hallows was built in 1166. The area is also associated with a megalithic burial ground, destroyed during seventeenth-century redevelopment.

As famous as Trinity College is the Bank of Ireland building at 2 College Green. The site's original occupant, Chichester House, was home to the first Irish parliament, which met in 1661. It was demolished in the 1720s to make way for the present-day building, but its future as the centre-piece of Irish legislative life came to an end in 1801, when the Act of Union rendered it politically redundant.

Bank of Ireland

The Bank of Ireland building, which dominates one side of College Green, and stares impassively towards Trinity College, has few rivals in Dublin when it comes to combining history, beauty and grandeur. When the Irish Parliament earned the distinction of voting itself out of existence in the 1801 Act of Union (helped, it must be added, by much English bribery and native greed), it rendered this building redundant, and put Ireland under the direct control of Westminster.

The building was subsequently sold to the Bank of Ireland with the instruction that the interior be altered to prevent the debating chamber from being used again for such a purpose. The original interior of the House of Commons was thus demolished, but the interior of the House of Lords survived, and remains the subject of much interest. The vaulted ceiling of the Lords chamber, complete with historical tapestries commemorating the Siege of Derry (1689) and the Battle of the Boyne (1690), together with a 1,233-piece chandelier, recall the chamber's former glories. The original 8-kg silver gilt mace of the Parliament was recovered from Christies of London by the Bank authorities in 1937, having been sold by the descendants of Speaker of Parliament John Foster. The Commons debating chamber is now the site of the main banking hall. The gallery, which once hosted audiences of 700 observers, is gone, and there is virtually nothing here to hint at the chamber's past.

The Act of Union had ended an exercise in Irish parliamentarianism begun by the Anglo-Irish ascendancy, which culminated in the Grattan Parliament of 1782. Henry Grattan himself still looks out across College Green and the city where he once proudly proclaimed, 'Ireland is now a nation.' Hopes that this site would be restored to its former use when the Republic gained independence were dashed when the fledgling Irish government decided to make Leinster House, on Kildare Street, the centre of democracy in Ireland. Among other reasons, it was felt that Leinster House was easier to defend.

The circular part of the building was designed by Edward Lovett Pearce and built between 1729 and 1739 as a bi-cameral house with an impressive colonnaded front. In 1785, Gandon, who was responsible for many of Dublin's most beautiful buildings, added the Corinthian portico on Westmoreland Street, as the entrance to the House of Lords, the Lords having objected to entering by the same route as mere Commons members.

The statues of Hibernia, Fidelity and Commerce stare down from above the forecourt, while over Gandon's entrance Wisdom, Justice and Liberty cast a cold eye on the proceedings below. The seemingly out-of-place sentry boxes, which still stand guard in the bank's forecourt, hark back to an era that ended just before the Second World War, when the bank retained its own guard of soldiers.

COPE STREET

A functional, rather than beautiful street, this was named for Robert Cope who married, during the mid-1700s, into the Fownes family, which was responsible for much of the area's development. Home to an assortment of merchants, Cope Street was hit by the construction of the Central Bank during the 1970s, when part of the street was demolished.

COPPER ALLEY

One of the most interesting streets in Temple Bar, the Alley derives its name from a Lady Alice Fenton, who lived there around 1600, and who used to hand out copper money for the poor of the area. Famous down through the years for its cobblers, taverns and printing houses, Copper Alley was also central to the life of the area, because of the access it allowed patrons of the Music Hall on Fishamble Street. When the throughway to Fishamble Street was closed off in the late 1800s, Copper Alley lost much of its trade and importance.

CORK HILL

Named for Richard Boyle, the First Earl of Cork in the mid 1600s, Cork Hill has had a chequered history both socially and architecturally. Originally lined with the mansions of the well-heeled of Dublin society, the street suffered from later development, when many of its buildings were demolished to make way for the building of the Royal Exchange and for the development of Parliament Street. The opening of Lord Edward Street also contributed to the demise of Cork Hill, in the same way that it spelled out the end of the good times for Copper Alley. Of note is the fact that the famous 'Hell Fire Club' was founded here in the Cork Hill Eagle Tavern.

CRAMPTON COURT
& CRAMPTON QUAY

Philip Crampton, who gave his name to the area, was in his time a book-dealer, city sheriff, and Lord Mayor of Dublin around the 1750s. He lived at Crampton Court and had the distinction of being credited with waging a 'war' on many of the gambling houses in the city at that time. Though it looks unlikely today, Crampton Court once boasted the main entrance to the Olympia Theatre. In the intervening years since it was laid down in 1745, the little laneway of Crampton Court has lost many of the houses and shops which once made it a busy quarter in Temple Bar. Nearby Crampton Quay is noteworthy only for being the shortest quay along the river, and for its tradition of book-sellers, still represented there today, albeit in much diminished number. One of the oldest candle-makers in the world, Rathborne Candles, was once based here; it is still in existence after five hundred years of the craft, though it has since moved to Dublin's East Wall.

CRANE LANE

This street owes its name to a public crane erected on the old Custom House Quay, and to the long-vanished docks and Custom House, located here in the 1600s. One of the most famous residents of the lane was *The Freeman's Journal*, which began printing its seditious material here in 1782. The laneway also hosted the city's first synagogue, built in the 1660s.

CROW STREET

After the suppression of the monasteries in 1537, the site of the Augustinian monastery which stood on what is now Cecilia Street and Crow Street was given to Walter Tyrrel, but eventually passed into the hands of William Crow, who lent his name to the street. His own home was in time turned over to accommodate Government offices and became known as

Crow's Nest. Now housing some of the best restaurants in Dublin, the street was formerly home to a number of well-known merchants and businesses, although perhaps its most notable inhabitant was the artist Hugh Douglas Hamilton, many of whose paintings hang in the National Gallery.

CROWN ALLEY

Once home to merchants and warehouses, Crown Alley has managed to retain its financial importance down to the present day, boasting bars and restaurants among its current residents. Though the southern end of the street, which connected Merchants' Arch and the Ha'penny Bridge to Dame Street, has long since disappeared, the street's location means that it remains at the very heart of the area. It is believed that the name derives from a tavern located here at one time.

Telephone Exchange

Originally built as Dublin's own telephone exchange, the building was completed at the turn of the century, and occupies a prime location, overlooking Temple Bar Square. It's one of the few buildings in Temple Bar still serving its original purpose, though these days the original operators have been replaced by a more modern, automatic exchange.

CURVED STREET

This brand-new street, which takes its name from its shape. links Temple Lane and Eustace Street and is home to the Temple Bar Music Centre.

DAME STREET

Forming the southernmost boundary of Temple Bar, Dame Street has, since it was laid down in the early 1600s, been one of the main avenues of Dublin City, travelling as it does from Dublin Castle and the City Hall at its western end to Trinity College at its easternmost point. Although today the Trinity College area is home to many of the city's financial institutions, the other end of the street boasts a number of Italian, Chinese and Thai restaurants, as well as the Olympia Theatre — and this from a street named after the Church of Mary del Dame around the 1380s, which itself was probably named in connection with a nearby dam, and originally built to serve local religious orders.

The Central Bank

For some, this is one of the most hated buildings in Dublin; for other people it is one of the best examples of modern architecture. For everyone, it's one of the most controversial structures in the Irish capital, as it towers above the surrounding streets and buildings. Constructed between 1972 and 1978, the Central Bank was built in a unique fashion, which is still evidenced by the present-day building. Each of its eight upper floors was raised from ground level by a system of cantilevers. Today, as well as its various financial and governmental roles, the Central Bank's forecourt provides a convenient meeting place for the hordes of local and international teenagers, who flood the city at the weekends.

Thomas Davis Memorial

The Davis memorial was the subject of much controversy when it was unveiled in 1966, but has since won over many of its detractors. Sculpted by Edward Delaney, the memorial depicts the poet and patriot Davis confronted by a fountain (dry these days) populated by the Heralds of the Four Irish Provinces.

Born in 1815, Davis died in 1845 at the youthful age of thirty. In his short life he had become a poet and a founder of *The Nation* — the voice of the Young Ireland movement who staged an abortive uprising.

The memorial stands near to the spot where an earlier statue of William III was blown up in 1929, having been defaced on numerous occasions by locals.

Henry Grattan Statue

This statue of Henry Grattan was created by the sculptor, John Henry Foley, who was also responsible for the twin Trinity College statues of Burke and Goldsmith, opposite which it stands; it has been pointed out by Dublin wits that the upraised arm of Grattan appears to be inviting the studious couplet to a party!

Born in nearby Temple Bar, Grattan was leader of the Liberal Party, and achieved a semi-independent parliament for the country. However, Grattan's Parliament lasted only a few years before it voted itself out of existence in the 1801 Act of Union. Erected in 1876, the statue reminds passers-by of the Bank of Ireland's splendid past. Ironically, this champion of the Irish cause was himself buried in Westminster Abbey in London.

The Olympia Theatre

Since opening its doors in 1749 as the 'Star of Erin Music Hall' the Olympia Theatre has played host to many of Ireland's greatest entertainers, musicians and actors, and has earned itself a number of names along the way. In 1817, following a complete rebuilding, it was called the 'Empire Theatre of Varieties', and at various times it has been known as the 'Palace Theatre' and as 'Dan Lowry's Music Hall'. But somewhere along the way, in between pantomimes and variety, plays and concerts, wars and independence, it came to be known as the 'Olympia'.

The second oldest theatre in Dublin and the only theatre in Temple Bar to survive from the eighteenth century, the Olympia has a reputation to be envied, and has in its time played host to stars such as Charlie Chaplin, Laurel and Hardy, Noël Coward and Jack Dee. Almost as famous as its performers have been its patrons, among whom was Peadar Kearney, the author of the Irish National Anthem. In 1915 Kearney turned the hoses on the unfortunate orchestra who had dared to play 'God Save the Queen'.

These days, the Olympia is known mainly for rock music gigs and comedy routines, but, as its colourful past would suggest, it also provides a splendid venue for theatre and variety, especially at Christmas and festival times.

ESSEX GATE
& ESSEX QUAY

Although the most imposing feature on Essex Quay is now the modern Dublin Corporation offices, the offices are not the first massive structure to have stood in this area. Essex Gate was built on the site of the strong-point of Buttevant's Tower, and linked the two ends — western and eastern — of Essex Street. At the eastern end of the quay, a second strong-point, Isolde's Tower, guarded the city. All remaining traces of the tower have been built upon, but it is commemorated by plaques and by the nearby bar, Isolde's Tower.

ESSEX STREET EAST

Named after Arthur Capel, Earl of Essex and a Lord Lieutenant of Ireland in the 1670s, Essex Street East continues to be one of the main arteries of Temple Bar. The fine buildings of the 1600s and 1700s may no longer house the well-heeled families they did in the past, but their future at least is assured as they are now home to many of the best-known art galleries of modern Temple Bar.

In fact, art has replaced printing as the main craft of the area. Essex Street East was formerly the site of numerous papers, including the *Dublin Gazette* of the seventeenth century, while George Faulkner, who published the books of Jonathan Swift (author of *Gulliver's Travels*), founded his printing works here.

Dolphin House

Though the heyday of the Dolphin Hotel has long since departed, it is still possible to judge the original beauty of the building from the elaborate stonework which still adorns the outside of it. Dolphin House, as it's now known, was built at the turn of the century, and enjoyed a healthy trade up to the 1970s. Then business declined and the hotel had vanished by the 1980s when the interior was sadly torn out to allow its conversion to the current courtroom facilities.

ESSEX STREET WEST

Though certainly not as busy a street as its more easterly namesake, Essex Street West has had its moments of notoriety — most notably, the presence of the Smock Alley Theatre, which was built in 1661. The theatre, famous for its boisterous acts and riotous audiences, had a chequered history until its demise in 1790. In 1671 three members of the public were killed when the galleries collapsed, while rioting among the audience left several dead in 1701, and wrecked the theatre in 1754.

EUSTACE STREET

Named after Sir Maurice Eustace, a former Lord Chancellor and Speaker of the House of Commons, Eustace Street is as famous for its religious history as it is for the bawdy bars which have lined its streets from the 1600s.

Both the Quakers and the Presbyterians have had strong links with this street since the early 1700s. The old Presbyterian School and Meeting House of 1715 still stand on Eustace Street, and the Quakers have maintained a presence there to the present day.

The street and its former bars, such as The Eagle, have strong links with Dublin and Irish history, particularly the period of 1798 and the rebellion of the United Irishmen. A plaque on the wall of the Friends Meeting House in Eustace Street commemorates the first meeting of the United Irishmen, who were inspired by the ideals of the French Revolution and who dreamt of an independent Ireland, free of religious intolerance. There is some dispute about exactly where The Eagle stood.

One of the more unusual sites in the street is the well of Saint Winifred, which was used by previous generations to draw fresh water from an underground source. The well had

been covered up, but was found by workmen laying cobble stones in 1991, and subsequently restored.

Irish Film Centre

Though you wouldn't think it to look at it now, the building which is home to the impressive Irish Film Centre was, up until a decade ago, the property of the Quakers, who have a long and honourable association with Dublin. The religious group has been in Temple Bar since the beginning of the 1700s, and at various points in Irish history its members have been to the fore in providing relief for the country's poor and hungry.

No. 6 Eustace Street was sold by the Quakers and subsequently became the Irish Film Centre, which opened in 1992. Something of an oasis of calm, the centre has two cinemas and contains the Irish Film Archive, while still remaining a quiet spot to relax over a coffee or a pint at any time of the day.

EXCHANGE STREET UPPER & LOWER

Taking its name from the City Hall, formerly the Royal Exchange, the street owes its narrow form to Dublin's medieval history. Three of the medieval city's strong-points — Case's Tower, Isolde's Tower and Buttevant's Tower — stood near here, while the curvature of the street follows accurately the path the old city walls would have taken.

Saints Michael and John's Church

Although it has been closed for worship for over a decade now, this church, which stands on the site of the Smock Alley

Theatre, was once central to the fight for the Emancipation of Catholics in Ireland.

In 1818, the bell of Saints Michael and John's was the first to ring out in three hundred years but, as the Penal Laws were still in place, a case was taken against the church to silence it again. The cause was taken up by one Daniel O'Connell, but the case was never heard, as it was dropped before it got to court.

The bell itself has survived intact, though it no longer peals out its call to worship. Facing out towards the Liffey, the Georgian building beside the church, which opened in 1813, was the old presbytery, while on the other side of the church is its former school.

FISHAMBLE STREET

Reputed to be the oldest street in the city, this was one of the most populous streets of Viking Dublin, and it now forms the western boundary of Temple Bar. The somewhat unusual name derives from the old fish stalls which at one time stood here, and the street can trace its connection to the fishmongering trade back as far as the early 1400s.

In common with Exchange Street, Fishamble Street has a long and rich medieval and Viking heritage. Christchurch Cathedral has stood here since 1170, but at one point a Viking church, dedicated to Saint Olaf, King of Norway, stood on the site.

More recently, the street was the preferred location of such Irish notables as Henry Grattan, and the poet James Clarence

Mangan, both of whom had homes here. Perhaps its most famous connection of all, however, is that concerning the composer, George Frederick Handel, who, in 1742, gave the first performance of his new composition in the famous Fishamble Street Music Hall.

Fishamble Street Music Hall

Designed by Richard Cassels, the Music Hall opened in 1741, and just a year later Handel, seeking a more appreciative audience than the one he had just abandoned in London, staged the first performance of his *Messiah* here. Over seven hundred people packed into the hall, the men without their swords and the ladies without their hoops, while the massed choirs of Saint Patrick's and Christchurch Cathedrals made up the chorus.

The Music Hall continued to thrive until the Act of Union, when it was sold, although its connection with entertainment continued until its take-over by an iron works in the late 1800s.

Today all that remains of the Music Hall is the entrance and the original door, which still forms part of Keenan's engineering works.

FLEET STREET

In the 1840s, Fleet Street was home to the Bavarian, Hamburg, Sardinian, Belgian, Portuguese and Ottoman consuls, but by the end of the century many of those consuls which still retained a presence in Dublin had moved to Ballsbridge.

A hospital for 'incurables' was situated here in the mid-1700s, and one of Ireland's most famous patriots, the young Kevin Barry who was hanged in 1920, was born in this street.

Like many nearby streets, Fleet Street probably derives its name from its counterpart in London.

FOSTER PLACE

One of the most intriguing though often ignored streets in Dublin, Foster Place is the cul-de-sac nestling beneath the gaze of the Bank of Ireland (formerly Parliament House) at College Green.

Named after John Foster, a speaker of the House of Commons, Foster Place was formerly known as Turnstile Alley but access between it and Fleet Street was finally closed off in 1928.

Allied Irish Banks

Though dwarfed by its larger and more illustrious Bank of Ireland neighbour, the Allied Irish Banks building can, at least, lay claim to the title of being the longest-running bank in the city. The building has operated under various names since it was first bought as a financial premises by Thomas Lighton in 1799, but since then it has always housed professionals working in the banking industry.

FOWNES STREET UPPER & LOWER

Fownes Street has had a chequered history; it has at times been home to wealthy merchants and commercial institutions, while at other times has become a popular site for many of the city's brothels.

It was named after Sir William Fownes, a former Lord Mayor of Dublin (1708) and Sheriff of Dublin, who owned and developed much of Temple Bar. Many of the streets in the area are named after members of his extended family.

Arthur Griffith, one of the founders of Sinn Féin, and one of the signatories, along with Michael Collins, of the Treaty which led to civil war and the partition of Ireland in the 1920s, had an office on Fownes Street where the *United Irishman* newspaper was published.

Though part of Fownes Street, like Cope Street, was demolished to make way for the building of the Central Bank in the 1970s, the street remains central to the daily life of the area.

LORD EDWARD STREET

Named for the 'citizen Lord' who lost his life when he became leader of the United Irishmen in the run-up to the 1798 rebellion, Lord Edward Street runs from Cork Hill to Christchurch Place.

A number of buildings in Cork Hill had to be demolished to make way for the new street, which resulted in the completion of one of Dublin's most charming avenues, running from Christchurch Cathedral through Lord Edward Street, Cork Hill and Dame Street to Trinity College and Parliament House in College Green.

Guide to Temple Bar

MEETING HOUSE SQUARE

Tucked away between Eustace Street and Sycamore Street, and accessible from the Irish Film Centre, this square hosts a food market every Saturday at which you can buy homemade breads, cheeses, chocolates, pasta sauces, drinks and other delicacies. In summer the IFC has outdoor film showings here.

MERCHANTS' ARCH

When the passageway was ordered in 1822 by the Wide Streets Commission in 1822, the Merchants' Guild requested that iron gates be placed at either end, to prevent 'instances of immorality in the night-time'. The request was denied, however, and the arch was constructed as originally planned. Whether the immorality ever came to pass is unclear, but Merchants' Arch today is one of the busiest and most charming thoroughfares in the city. For many people, locals and tourists alike, there's no prettier way to enter Temple Bar than to cross the Ha'penny Bridge at night and walk through the Merchants' Arch.

Though there is little room for shops there, Merchants' Arch, like a number of the streets in Temple Bar, became home at the start of the century to bookshops, and, like Crampton Court, the passageway featured in James Joyce's work, in no less a book than *Ulysses*.

Merchants' Hall (Front entrance Crampton Quay)

Though it has lost some of its glory these days, it is still possible to glimpse how important this building was when it

was home to the most important of the city's guilds — that of the Merchants. Built in 1821, the Hall was abandoned by its owners when the Dublin Guilds disappeared in the 1840s, the victims of politics and new legislation. Since then it has hosted a variety of occupants, including individual merchants, missionaries, and currently a fast-food joint downstairs and a nightclub upstairs.

Ha'penny Bridge

A cast-iron bridge, built in 1816, the Ha'penny or Halfpenny Bridge retains a unique place in the hearts of locals, and remains one of the central symbols of the city. Like many of Dublin's other bridges, it has enjoyed a variety of names, including Wellington Bridge and Metal Bridge, but was officially named the Liffey Bridge in 1922. The name Ha'penny has its origins in the halfpenny toll which was imposed upon those using it to cross the river, right up to around the time of the First World War. There was once a sentry-type box at each end of the bridge to house the two toll collectors, part of whose job it was to prevent horses from using the bridge.

The bridge reportedly owes its origins to a local ferry man who reckoned it a better business proposition to build a bridge than repair or replace his ferries.

PARLIAMENT ROW
& PARLIAMENT STREET

Not to be confused with each other, these two are situated at opposite ends of Temple Bar. Most people know of the existence of Parliament Street, but few take the time to note Parliament Row. Both streets owe their names to Parliament Buildings. But whereas Parliament Street is one of the busiest in the area, lined with fashionable restaurants and trendy bars as it makes its way from the river to City Hall, Parliament Row has become a forgotten, rather unattractive cul-de-sac.

The death-knell for the Row, which ran from Fleet Street to College Green, was sounded when the Bank Armoury was built, and the street was finally closed off in the late 1920s. Originally known as Turnstile Alley, it couldn't survive being blocked, whereas the upper end of the street, modern-day Foster Place, has prospered and managed to retain its charm.

Parliament Street, on the other hand, was the first street to be built by the Wide Streets Commission in 1757. Though most Dubliners now extol the virtues of the Commission, it was in fact detested at the time by locals, who resented the compulsory purchase orders used to evict them from their squalid homes. Many of those who ignored orders had their roofs removed overnight to force them to leave.

Thomas Read & Co., Parliament Street

Few people get to leave Temple Bar without finding out that Read's is the oldest shop in Dublin. In a tradition begun by

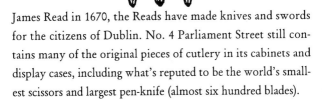

James Read in 1670, the Reads have made knives and swords for the citizens of Dublin. No. 4 Parliament Street still contains many of the original pieces of cutlery in its cabinets and display cases, including what's reputed to be the world's smallest scissors and largest pen-knife (almost six hundred blades).

Sunlight Chambers, Parliament Street

One of the most charming buildings in Dublin, Sunlight Chambers is simultaneously one of the dirtiest. Built for the Lever Brothers at the turn of the century, and named after their brand of Sunlight soap, the eye is drawn to the beautiful bas-relief frieze, showing working men making their clothes dirty, and women washing them and making them clean.

A family business, which has since become the giant Unilever multinational company famous for making a wide variety of products, the company has to date been luckier than its former building, although to have survived through decades of demolition is no mean feat.

PRICE'S LANE

More of an access street than anything else, Price's Lane dates from the 1700s. A handy way of moving from the quays to Fleet Street, Price's Lane was once home to the Royal Assurance Company's own horse-drawn fire brigade.

SYCAMORE STREET

Linking Dame Street to Essex Street East, Sycamore Street takes its name, predictably enough, from the tree of the same name, and roughly follows the east bank of the underground Poddle River en route to the Liffey. In previous times, tenement housing lined one side of the street, while the Olympia took up much of the other side. Of the tradesmen who worked here, gold-beaters seem to have been prominent, but again printers are in evidence. Of interest too was the opening of Bewley's first coffee house in 1846 in numbers 19 and 20 Sycamore Alley, as it was then known.

TEMPLE BAR

Named after William Temple, this street had the distinction in the seventeenth century of having two ferry crossings — at the bottom of Temple Lane and near Fownes Street.

Stretching from Fleet Street to Essex Street East, Temple Bar can lay claim to some of the most popular (and best) bars and restaurants in the area. The art of providing rest and comfort for weary travellers is a much practised one on this street, which has enjoyed a long association with taverns and bars.

Striking a rather different note, however, is its association with violin makers; though they have since departed, they were once a common sight in the street.

TEMPLE LANE

Up until the 1720s, this street enjoyed the rather unfortunate name of 'Dirty Lane', which by all accounts was an accurate description of it in those times. Times change, however, and Temple Lane has taken its place, if not in the sun, then at least alongside the other throughways and roads of Temple Bar. Today the street is the site of numerous restaurants and businesses, as well as the excellent Temple Lane Studios.

Temple Lane Studios

Now a vibrant recording studio, No. 11 originally started life as a tea and wine store — a typical enough location for such activities given the proliferation of merchants in the area. One of the properties bought by the CIÉ transport company as part of its plans to turn Temple Bar into a city station, the building was spared such an unfortunate fate, and today is one of the jewels in the crown of Temple Bar.

WELLINGTON QUAY

Named for that most reluctant of Irishmen, Arthur Wellesley, the Duke of Wellington, this quay commemorates his victory over Napoleon at the battle of Waterloo in 1815. One of the most impressive waterfronts in the city, Wellington Quay has long been a favourite haunt of solicitors. It is also home to the Clarence Hotel,

The Clarence Hotel

One of the properties enjoying a new lease of life since the rejuvenation of Temple Bar, the Clarence Hotel boasts as its owners U2's Bono and The Edge, who have spent millions turning the hotel into one of the more stylish in the city.

Without doubt one of most pleasant buildings along the quays, the Clarence has long since shed its shabby image of the

1980s and is an impressive tenant on the site once occupied by Dublin's original Custom House, built around 1700.

The newly refurbished Clarence has kept faith with many of the old traditions and still has the old octagonal bar, popular with many locals. If you can't afford the £1,500 (circa) penthouse, complete with outdoor hot-tub overlooking the roofs of Temple Bar, you might at least enjoy the splendour of the award-winning tea-rooms.

Access to the hotel is also from Essex Street East, where patrons of The Kitchen, U2's night-club, can be spotted in their natural nocturnal habitat, queuing at the entrance.

WESTMORELAND STREET

Another street named for an earl, Westmoreland Street shares with D'Olier Street the distinction of being the last major road laid down by the Wide Streets Commissioners. One of the most important streets in modern Dublin, it was constructed in 1801 to serve O'Connell Bridge, originally built as Carlisle Bridge in 1798.

Bewley's Café

Famous for its teas and coffees, Bewley's has long enjoyed a special relationship with the people of Dublin. The original name of the café can still be seen on the side of the Westmoreland Street building which grandly states Bewley's Oriental Café.

The chain was begun in the 1840s when Joshua Bewley, a Quaker newly arrived from England, opened his first tea shop near the site of the present-day Olympia Theatre. The Westmoreland Street Café opened in 1916 and became something of a centre of fashion for Dubliners, who arrived in their carriages to be helped down by the café's attendant doorman. The recent opening of The Bridge, a bar and music venue, downstairs in the building, has managed to recapture some of that early popularity, and though the doormen may not be as accommodating as their forerunners, the atmosphere more than compensates.

The Westmoreland Street café has survived despite widespread damage caused by a fire in the 1970s, and the collapse of part of the ceiling in the 1980s. The family connection ended only in 1986, when the chain was sold. Prior to that it had been part of the Bewley's tradition that the staff held shares in the business. Since its take-over, the chain has run profitably, opening new stores across Ireland and abroad, even as far away as Japan.

Part Two

Shopping

ABOUT FACE
20 Temple Lane South
Health and skincare shop for men.

AN TÁIN
13 Temple Bar
Men's and women's clothing with a distinctly Celtic flavour. You can buy knitwear, linen and designer wear here costing from as little as £10 to over £300. Proves that small is beautiful.

BORDERLINE
17 Temple Bar
Good place to dig out old, rare and unusual records as well as the newer stuff.

BYRNE'S TEMPLE BAR LTD
Essex Street East
Fresh meat and ready-cooked meals.

CAFÉ INN
6 Parliament Street
Sells retail and wholesale, wide range of coffees and teas.

Shopping

CLADDAGH RECORDS
2 Cecilia Street
Tremendous range of traditional Irish music, as well as world, bluegrass and country music.

COMET RECORDS
5 Cope Street
Good stock of Indy and dance music, as well as decent coverage of new Irish bands.

CONNOLLY BOOKS
43 Essex Street East
Another landmark in Temple Bar, Connolly Books has an excellent collection of Irish history, and a wide range of political books, including some by James Connolly himself.

CROWN JEWELS
5 Crown Alley
Fashion accessories.

DUBLIN SCHOOL OF ENGLISH
10 Westmoreland Street
English language school for foreign students.

THE EAGER BEAVER
17 Crown Alley
Huge selection of second-hand clothes. Also offers discounts to students, unemployed and the elderly.

ERROL LITTLE OPTOMETRIST
26 Wellington Quay
Eyecare.

ETNIKA
Temple Bar Square
Accessories.

EYECON ESSENTIAL EYEWEAR
Spranger's Yard, Fownes Street
Fashion for the eye-conscious.

FLIP/HELTER SKELTER
4 Fownes Street Upper
Retro clothing from the 1950s, 1960s and 1970s. Club gear too.

THE FLYING PIG
17 Crow Street
Good place to find those fantasy/sci-fi books you've been looking for.

GLYCINE OF SWITZERLAND
Eustace Street
Watch shop, selling new watches and repairing older ones.

KC CONFECTIONERY/BAKERY
18 Westmoreland Street
Fresh bread and cakes.

THE NATURE WORKS

Spranger's Yard, Crow Street

Health foods, wholefoods, natural cosmetics.

O'CONNELL'S PHARMACY

17 Westmoreland Street

Dispensing chemist.

PADANIA GASTRONOMIC EMPORIUM

Spranger's Yard, Crow Street

Exclusive Italian delicacies.

PATRICK CLEERE ANGLING AND SHOOTING

5 Bedford Row

House of Hardy appointed agent, selling hunting and fishing equipment.

PULSE FITNESS

1 Temple Bar

Work off the night before the morning after at this fitness club.

RORY'S FISHING TACKLE

17 Temple Bar

A veritable institution in the area, the shop has been in Temple Bar for more than three decades.

SHARPESVILLE/REAL MCCOY

3 Fownes Street Upper

Second-hand and new clothing, as well as trendier fashions.

SKATE CITY
14 Crown Alley
Skates and trendy sports clothing for the young at heart.

SOCCER CITY
Ha'penny Bridge
One of the best collections of soccer gear, and memorabilia in the country.

SQUARE WHEEL CYCLE WORKS
Dublin Resource Centre, 21 Temple Lane
Bike and bike repair shop.

TABOO
Spranger's Yard
Jewellery and accessories.

THE TEMPLE BAR FOOD MARKET
Meeting House Square
Run only on a Saturday, the market is a chance for Irish food specialists to show off their wares. The quality is good, and you can sample the delights on offer although some of the stalls can be expensive. Still, a very good way to spend a Saturday afternoon.

TEMPLE BAR OPTICIAN
41 Wellington Quay
Specialises in 1950, 1960s and 1970s eyewear.

TEMPLE BAR PHARMACY

21 Essex Street East

Dispensing chemist.

VIRGIN MEGASTORE

Aston Quay

A huge store, selling all kinds of music, videos, games and related paraphernalia.

Part Three

Art and Culture

AFRICA CALLS GALLERY
2 Temple Lane South. Tel: (+353 1) 671 5107
Zimbabwean Stone Sculpture and Handicrafts.

THE ARK
Eustace Street. Tel: (+353 1) 670 7788
One of the true jewels in the Temple Bar crown, this is an arts
centre for children with work by children.

ARTHOUSE
Curved Street. Tel: (+353 1) 605 6800
A rather trendy multi-media centre, the Arthouse is used for
exhibitions, but also has an Internet café. The building is home
to a creative studio, a digital skills training centre and the Arts
Information Bureau.

BANK OF IRELAND ARTS CENTRE
Foster Place. Tel: (+353 1) 671 1488
The story of banking may not be everybody's idea of excite-
ment, but the BOI Arts Centre charts the role and development
of the profession in Ireland over the past two centuries.

DESIGNYARD

12 Essex Street East. Tel: (+353 1) 677 8467

Now home to the Contemporary Jewellery Gallery, DESIGNyard houses a huge range of Irish crafts and arts. As a result of its co-operation with the Crafts Council of Ireland, the building is home to some of the best cutting-edge Irish craft and design currently available.

DUBLIN'S VIKING ADVENTURE

Essex Street West. Tel: (+353 1) 679 6949

The adventure centre tells a cracking good yarn that should appeal to all of the family. As well as tracing the important role played by the Vikings in the development and life of Dublin, the centre hosts an Irish evening of traditional music, singing and dancing. There's also a restaurant and craft shop.

THE GAIETY SCHOOL OF ACTING

Meeting House Square. Tel: (+353 1) 679 9277

Though it enjoys a reasonably low profile outside the thespian world, this is one of the country's leading acting schools. Founded in 1986, the school carries on the long, proud association Temple Bar has had with the performing arts.

GALLERY OF PHOTOGRAPHY

Meeting House Square. Tel: (+353 1) 671 4654

The only gallery in the country devoted entirely to the art of the photograph, the gallery regularly hosts unusual collections and works. Check out its postcards and book stocks. Chances are that if it's hard-hitting or controversial, it will be on display here first. If you prefer, you can just enjoy the award-winning architecture. Seminars and workshops are also run here.

GRAPHIC STUDIO GALLERY

Off Cope Street. Tel: (+353 1) 679 8021

This is the oldest gallery in Dublin dealing in contemporary original prints by both recognised and emerging Irish artists.

IRISH FILM CENTRE

Eustace Street. Tel: (+353 1) 679 5744

This old Quaker meeting house was redesigned to house two cinemas, the Irish Film Archive, and film education facilities. Regularly used for exhibitions and festivals, the IFC also has a bar and restaurant, and its relaxed atmosphere makes it a good place to meet. It also shows good, non-mainstream movies.

OLYMPIA THEATRE

Dame Street. Tel: (+353 1) 677 7744

The grand old lady of Temple Bar, the Olympia still forms the main event in many people's weekly social calendar. These days, it hosts live music as well as stand-up comedy gigs.

ORIGINAL PRINT GALLERY
Black Church Studio, 4 Temple Bar.
Tel: (+353 1) 677 3657

If wood-cuts, silk-screens, etchings or lithographs get you hot under the collar, then you'd best be sure to take a trip to this gallery. The contemporary handmade products represent superb quality and craftsmanship. The work on view is produced by a wide variety of Irish artists.

STICKS AND STONES GALLERY AND GIFTS
8 Crow Street. Tel: (+353 1) 672 5438

This friendly gallery presents original artworks by new and established artists. Traditional craft techniques are strongly featured, especially bogwood sculpture and jewellery, ceramics and tapestry weavings. Unusual gift items are also available. In addition, the gallery features acoustic music sessions on Sunday afternoons.

TEMPLE BAR GALLERY AND STUDIOS
5-9 Temple Bar. Tel: (+353 1) 671 0073

This is the largest studio and gallery complex in Ireland. Get lost in here as you browse, looking at the constantly changing and interesting exhibitions. Painting, drawing, sculpture and photography are all represented in this gallery, originally set up to help new, emerging Irish artists.

Art and Culture

Art and Culture

TEMPLE BAR MUSIC CENTRE

Curved Street. Tel: (+353 1) 670 9202

Though young, happening and loud doesn't fit everyone's idea of a good night out, the music centre is one of the most popular venues in Temple Bar for the youth of today. There's a club, a music venue, a café, a bar and a fantastic week-long programme, together with pleasant and helpful staff.

Clubs and Entertainment

BAD BOB'S
Essex Street East
A great spot for late-night entertainment, Bad Bob's specialises in live music and fast service. The music's usually rock or American honky-tonk, while the food's filling. If you can make it there early enough, you can avoid the cover charge.

BOOMERANG NIGHT CLUB
Aston Place
Loud music and a young crowd.

CLUB M
Anglesea Street
At the back of Bloom's Hotel, Club M is a good nightclub if you can get past the bouncers. Again, a young crowd, but the music and atmosphere are both good.

DUBLIN'S LEFT BANK BAR
Anglesea Street
With traditional music on a regular basis, the Left Bank is a good place for a pint and a bit of craic.

Clubs & Entertainment

EAMON DORAN'S
Crown Alley
One of the best-known venues in Dublin, Doran's offers a variety of live rock music, and there's a club upstairs. Though the bands featured here may never reach stardom, most of them take their music seriously.

FITZSIMONS BAR
Essex Street East
More traditional music, and a good bar.

THE FURNACE
Aston Place
Plastic glasses, cheap beer and decent bands are the main attractions of this club run by the Union of Students in Ireland for students from anywhere.

HA'PENNY BRIDGE INN
Wellington Quay
There's a weekly comedy gig on in this great little boozer — well worth catching if you can make it. Otherwise there's plenty of traditional music and good humour on offer.

ISOLDE'S
Essex Street West
One of the newer clubs in Temple Bar, Isolde's has proven itself a hit with late-night revellers and party-goers. The music is mainly clubby, but the atmosphere is one of the best in town.

THE KITCHEN

Essex Street East

Located beneath the Clarence Hotel, the Kitchen is the famous nightclub owned by the even more famous U2. Definitely well worth a visit just to say you were there— if you can out-wait the usual hordes standing at the door.

OLIVER ST JOHN GOGARTY'S

Temple Bar

A great spot for a pint, this bar is also a staging post for one of the city's literary pub crawls. It also hosts a great traditional music programme, throughout the week, which is enjoyed by both tourists and locals alike.

THE OLYMPIA THEATRE

Dame Street

'Midnight at the Olympia' remains one of the best gigs in Dublin at the weekend. The atmosphere is relaxed — everyone's there to party and have a good time — and the venue itself smacks of style, even if its days of splendour are behind it. If you're lucky, you might even stumble upon a big-name band slumming it for the night. On the right night, the Olympia can beat any venue in Dublin when it comes to hosting gigs.

THE PIER NITE-CLUB

Eustace Street

A very popular night club, the Pier is definitely for the young at heart. The music is loud, though fans claim it's also the best around, while the dancing is frenetic. Again, you have to get past the bouncers and through the front door first.

THE TEMPLE BAR MUSIC CENTRE

Curved Street

Purpose built to serve the needs of the musical youth of today, the music centre is the best music venue in Temple Bar, offering a solid week-long programme of gigs and events.

Part Five

Accommodation

This is intended as a rough guide to the accommodation available in Temple Bar and its cost. Prices will vary from low to high season and may be changed without notice. Similarly, many hotels will offer deals and special rates, which will change from season to season.

ASTON HOTEL
Aston Quay. Tel: (+353 1) 677 9300
Overlooking the Liffey, the Aston Hotel is in an enviable location right at the heart of the city. There are 25 bedrooms, all en suite, and all with television, telephone and coffee facilities.

High Season: from £40 per person sharing

Low Season: from £30 per person sharing

Single room occupancy carries a supplement charge

BARNACLE'S TEMPLE BAR HOUSE
Cecilia Street. Tel: (+353 1) 671 6277
One of the best of the new tourist hostels, Barnacle's rooms are all en suite, though a little on the snug side. Good security and all the usual facilities, including a self-catering kitchen, a common room with television and music, a laundry and a shop.

Guide to Temple Bar

From £15 per person sharing a double room
From £10 per person sharing a four, six, eight or ten-bed room
(Above prices apply to Low Season)

BEWLEY'S HOTEL
Fleet Street. Tel: (+353 1) 670 8122
Attached to the Westmoreland Street café, the entrance to this
hotel is on Fleet Street. Though the hotel business is a relatively
new venture for Bewley's, their experience in service is clearly
of huge benefit to them. The hotel is located at the edge of
Temple Bar, near Westmoreland Street and O'Connell Bridge.
Single rooms from £78
Double rooms from £98

BLOOM'S HOTEL
Anglesea Street. Tel: (+353 1) 671 5622
One of the best-known hotels in Dublin, Bloom's has become
something of a landmark in Temple Bar. The hotel has 86
rooms, with all of the usual facilities, and has a bar, restaurant
and very hip club attached to it as well.
Single rooms from £90
Doubles rooms from £110

THE CLARENCE HOTEL
Wellington Quay. Tel: (+353 1) 670 9000
Without doubt the most fashionable place to stay in Temple
Bar, the Clarence has enjoyed a renaissance since millions of

pounds worth of investment money was poured into it by the local boys made good, U2. The hotel is ultra-stylish, and all rooms are en suite with video, candles, and Egyptian linen. The hotel boasts the aptly named Octagon bar, an award-winning restaurant, a Tea Rooms, and U2's nightclub — the Kitchen. Among other celebs, Tina Turner has stayed here, but the hotel prefers not to flag its high-profile customers.

Rooms begin at around £100, but if you fancy a night in the Penthouse, complete with baby grand piano and outdoor hot-tub overlooking Temple Bar, be prepared to write a cheque for around £1,450.

THE GEORGE FREDERIC HANDEL HOTEL

16 Fishamble Street. Tel: (+353 1) 670 9400

Situated on one of Dublin's oldest streets, this hotel boasts its own popular bar and restaurant, as well as the usual hotel facilities.

Single rooms from £70

Double rooms from £100

THE HARDING HOTEL

Copper Alley. Tel: (+353 1) 679 6500

Located right beside Christchurch Cathedral, the Harding Hotel is a new hotel with 53 bedrooms, all of which have en suite facilities, telephones and television. Great views of the Cathedral, and there's a good bar and café.

High Season: £50 for a single room

Low Season: £45 for a single room

KINLAY HOUSE

Lord Edward Street. Tel: (+353 1) 679 6644

Renowned as one of Dublin's best and oldest budget accommodation sites, Kinlay House offers a variety of single, twin and four/six-bedded rooms, along with left-luggage facilities, self-catering kitchens, TV lounges and laundry facilities for the budget traveller.

High Season: £18 for a single room

Low Season: £17.50 for a single room

Dorms from £9 per person sharing

THE MORGAN

Fleet Street. Tel: (+353 1) 679 3939

Another new hotel in the area, the Morgan is not aimed at the budget traveller. The emphasis in this hotel is on design and style. The bedrooms are equipped with a CD player and video, as well as television. Security includes in-room safes. Internet access and ISDN lines are also available.

Single rooms from £95

Double rooms from £120

OLIVER ST JOHN GOGARTY'S TEMPLE BAR HOSTEL

Anglesea Street. Tel: (+353 1) 671 1822

A good bet for those seeking budget accommodation, this hostel is right in the heart of the area. Its rooms are all en suite, and the pub next door sells good traditional Irish food at a discount price for guests of the hostel.

Double rooms from £16 per person sharing

Triple and four-bed rooms are also available

Dorms from £12 per person sharing

(Above prices apply to weekdays in the Low Season)

PARAMOUNT HOTEL

Parliament Street & Essex Gate. Tel: (+353 1) 677 9062

Opening in August 1999, this hotel retains the original façade, which at night is bathed in light. Inside it evokes the 1930s but is thoroughly modern, with simple and elegant furniture and fittings. All the usual facilities, including its own bistro and bar.

Two-night weekend breaks from £90 per person

Three-night midweek breaks from £105 per person

THE PARLIAMENT HOTEL

Lord Edward Street. Tel: (+353 1) 670 8777

This hotel has one of the best locations in Dublin, fronting on the entrance to Dublin Castle. There are 63 rooms en suite, all with the usual facilities, and there's a bar and restaurant as well.

Single rooms from £90

Double rooms from £120

(Above prices apply to the Low Season)

THE RIVER HOUSE HOTEL

Eustace Street. Tel: (+353 1) 670 7655

With 29 rooms, all en suite and with their own television and telephone facilities, the River House Hotel is well suited to anyone wishing to stay in the Temple Bar area. Danger Doyle's bar is attached to the hotel, and there's also a night-club for the young at heart.

Single rooms from £49

Double rooms from £60

(Above prices apply to the Low Season)

TEMPLE BAR HOTEL

Fleet Street. Tel: (+353 1) 677 3333

One of the best-known hotels in Temple Bar, this has 130 bedrooms en suite, with television, telephones and usual facilities.

There's a popular bar and cocktail lounge downstairs, as well as meeting-room facilities.

Single rooms from £99

Double rooms from £130

THE TRINITY ARCH HOTEL
Dame Street. Tel: (+353 1) 679 4455

Housed in one of the most beautiful buildings along Dame Street, the Trinity Arch Hotel is one of Temple Bar's newest accommodation centres. There are 29 rooms en suite, and the hotel also has two bars and a restaurant.

Single rooms from £65

Double rooms from £100

THE WELLINGTON HOTEL
Wellington Quay. Tel: (+353 1) 677 9315

Another hotel with river-views, the Wellington can offer visitors a location right in the centre of Temple Bar. It has a popular bar and restaurant downstairs and also a nightclub.

Single rooms from £50

Double rooms from £90

Part Six

Food and Drink

ABRAKEBABRA

Westmoreland Street and Merchant's Arch

Despite the exotic name, this is fast food Irish-style, with chips and kebabs providing the mainstay of the patrons here. A favourite, post-pub-closing-time haunt for locals.

AFSANA

3 Temple Lane South. Tel: 679 9833

Tandoori restaurant offering good-quality, reasonably priced food. This restaurant will serve you well, whether you're simply after a quiet night out or are travelling in a group.

Main course from £7 to £10

APACHE PIZZA

Dame Street. Tel: 677 1888

No need to book at this sit-in or take-away pizza place. Popular with the young and those in need of a fast bite.

THE ALAMO

Temple Bar. Tel: 677 6546

Well known and much loved for its reasonable prices and its

spicy Mexican food, the Alamo can be either the last port of call for revellers or the main event for diners. Very popular with students and locals, the dishes are tasty and inexpensive.

Main course from £4 to £7

AR VICOLETTTO
Crow Street. Tel: 670 8662

Small, homely Italian osteria with a family-run atmosphere and a Roman flavour to the authentic cuisine. There's also a good selection of wines, but reservations are necessary at busy times.

Main course from £5 to £10

THE AULD DUBLINER
17 Anglesea Street

One of the best-known bars, the Auld Dubliner often fills up early in the evening, so make sure you go early. A good place to pass the time if you're waiting for a table in nearby Elephant & Castle. Try to beat a path upstairs to see the painted ceilings of the upper bar. Regular traditional music sessions.

AURIGA
6 Temple Bar Square. Tel: 671 8228

Mediterranean and European cuisine is the order of the day at this highly rated restaurant which has an enviable location at Temple Bar Square.

Main course from £9 to £14.

IL BACCARO

Meeting House Square. Tel: 671 4597

Another Italian location, but the emphasis here is on atmosphere as much as on the food. Set in one of the most enviable venues in Temple Bar, the low, curved ceilings of this cellar set the perfect atmosphere for a spot of wine-drinking and convivial subterfuge. The food is some of the most unusual Italian fare served in Dublin. It is generally packed so arrive early and get a good seat, then stay in it!

Main course from £6 to £12

BAD ASS CAFÉ

9-11 Crown Alley. Tel: 679 5981

As any Dubliner worth their salt will tell you, Sinéad O'Connor once worked here as a waitress, bustling tables. A pasta and pizza joint, which sells beer and wine as well, the Bad Ass is still one of the better places to eat in Temple Bar. Spot the overhead pulley, which shoots your order across the warehouse-style floor. It's usually packed with tourists and locals alike, so arrive early or you could be disappointed.

Main course from £5 to £10

BAD BOB'S

Essex Street East

Definitely one of the spots to hit if you're out for a night on the town, Bad Bob's specialises in live music of the loud variety. A bit of a mix of music venue, pub and restaurant, this is

Food and Drink

a popular spot for late-night tipplers. The average age here is a little older than at many of the other night-clubs around town, probably because of the music, which tends to be rock-oriented downstairs, while upstairs it's powered by chart-tracks. If you arrive late, you'll have to queue and pay a cover charge.

BESHOFF'S

14 Westmoreland Street. Tel: 677 8026

Another Dublin institution, this fish and chip shop was founded by Ivan Beshoff, one of the survivors of the mutiny of the Russian battleship *Potemkin* in 1905. Like its owner, the very Victorian building has managed to survive admirably in the face of wholesale destruction and architectural vandalism around it. The fish and chips aren't bad either, and are a

welcome change from the fare in the many burger chains
threatening to over-run other parts of Dublin.

BEWLEY'S

Westmoreland Street

You can't get much more of a Dublin classic than this.
Although its reputation is mainly for the range of teas and
coffees it sells, you can buy just about any kind of meal here,
whether it's a pick-me-up cup of tea, a scone or a traditional
Irish breakfast. Because of its location and popularity you
might find yourself having to queue for something to eat, but
when you make it to a table, you'll discover that there are few
better places in which to relax.

BOTTICELLI'S

3 Temple Bar. Tel: 672 7289

Authentic and reasonable Italian food ensure that Botticelli's
remains among the better restaurants in Temple Bar. The wine
list vies with the food for top honours while the atmosphere is
tasteful and straightforward. You can even enjoy a little low-
key live music with your meal.

Main course from £5 to £12

THE BRIDGE

Westmoreland Street

Part of Bewley's, which it flanks on both sides, The Bridge is a
two-storey affair, the ground floor being right beside Bewley's

Food and Drink

and serving coffee and food, while the other floor is underground and hosts regular live bands. The downstairs part is probably the more interesting; a warren of passageways and secluded seating areas allows couples or groups to remain out of sight, although never out of earshot of the music.

BROGAN'S BAR
Dame Street

Located beside the Olympia Theatre, this old establishment is a handy spot if you're on your way to a music gig in the theatre itself, or if you just fancy a quiet afternoon pint.

BRUNO'S
30 Essex Street East Tel: 670 6767

A more recent addition to Temple Bar's line-up of Italian restaurants, Bruno's has quickly earned itself a reputation for good food and a convivial atmosphere. Whether you're after inventive Italian/Mediterranean food, or just want to dine in pleasant surroundings, you'll find what you're looking for here. As it's another popular spot, make sure you book a table, and leave a little room for the desserts.

Main course from £10 to £16

BUSKER'S
Fleet Street

Populated mainly by young revellers who like loud music, Busker's enjoys a reputation for being both popular and trendy. It's probably not the best option if you're after a quiet pint, but it's a good bar for a night out, and for some it's just a great place to hang out in.

CAFÉ GERTRUDE

3 Bedford Row. Tel: 677 9043

A very pleasant café which serves good food, Café Gertrude is perfect for anyone wanting to get away from the hustle and bustle of the main parts of Temple Bar. A good place to relax and linger as long as you like.

CAFÉ INN

Parliament Street

Situated in the vicinity of the City Hall, Café Inn is a good spot to relax, enjoy a cuppa, and watch the world — and city councillors — go by.

CAFÉ IRIE

Fownes Street

A café with a young crowd and a chilled atmosphere, Irie serves hot sandwiches, soup, coffee and snacks designed to bolster flagging spirits. Also serves great wholefood.

CAFÉ LEOPOLD

Anglesea Street

Part of Bloom's Hotel, this large bar mainly hosts guests at the hotel, although it does have live music at times. A pleasant spot to have a quiet drink.

Guide to Temple Bar

CENTRAL PERCS
Essex Street East. Tel: 670 4193

It shouldn't be hard for any visiting New Yorkers (or *Friends* fans from anywhere) to guess the origins of this café's name. The absence of a park doesn't seem to have dented the café's popularity though, and inside you can relax with a coffee or order something more substantial from the restaurant menu.

THE CHAMELEON
1 Fownes Street Lower. Tel: 671 0362

Specialising in Indonesian cuisine, the Chameleon has a friendly atmosphere perfect for couples or families. The restaurant has table d'hôte menus costing in the region of £17, and specialises in interesting vegetarian dishes. Try the rijstaffel.

CHARLIE'S FAST FOOD
Dame Street. Tel: 679 3455

A Chinese eatery which won't slow you down if you're on a night out, or just want a quick bite after a night on the town. Food for around £5.

CIBO
Crown Alley. Tel: 671 7288

Informed dining in the heart of Temple Bar. With pizzas, pastas, steaks and a seasonal fish menu, there's something for everyone.

Main course from £6 to £10.

THE CRANE

Crane Lane

You could almost miss this pub, hidden away as it is. Not much of a surprise to learn that it's a quiet bar, with a mainly business-type crowd.

CYBERIA

Arthouse Multi-media Centre, Curved Street

Internet Café.

DANGER DOYLE'S

Eustace Street

Right in the heart of Temple Bar, Doyle's is usually populated by a younger crowd, keen on sampling the delights of the nearby music centre and the film centre. At the same time, it's a good spot for a quiet pint. Not at all dangerous.

DANIEL O'CONNELL

Aston Quay

Perched right on the corner of O'Connell Bridge, the Daniel O'Connell has managed to retain much of its regular crowd, unlike many of its neighbours in the area, but it does get some tourist trade because of its central location.

DA PINO

38–40 Parliament Street. Tel: 671 9308

Located on one of two sites where the original Hell Fire Club Main may have been located, there's little chance of Da Pino ever being allowed to fade into the background. One of the best-known Italian eateries in Temple Bar, the restaurant serves good food at low prices. A warm atmosphere complements the food, and Da Pino has a wide selection of beers to wash it down.

Main course from £5 to £12

DARKEY KELLY'S
Copper Alley

Hiding away on the very edge of Temple Bar, Darkey Kelly's is a nice stop-off point for those who are finding the hill tough-going. Popular with locals and tourists, this is one of the few bars in the area with a large screen where sports events are shown regularly.

DISH
Crow Street. Tel: 671 1248

Serving international food, this elegant restaurant is open all week round, with both lunch and dinner menus available. Some of the best food in Temple Bar, including a tasty Sunday brunch.

Main course from £10 to £15

DYFLINS
23 Temple Bar. Tel: 677 8528

Dyflins has a wide-ranging menu, but with an obvious Italian leaning.

Main course from £5 to £12

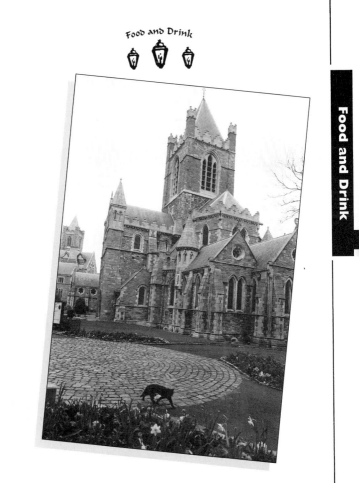

EAMON DORAN'S IMBIBING EMPORIUM
3A Crown Alley. Tel: 679 9773

Whether you fancy a good steak sandwich or a complete four-course dinner, Doran's offers value for money. Not only a restaurant but also a bar and a music venue. Patrons are spoiled for choice with what's on offer.

Main course from £6 to £14

EDDIE ROCKET'S

Dame Street

Fast food at a slightly more sedate pace, Eddie Rocket's American-style diner and burger joint provides decent American-style fare at a reasonable price.

EDEN

Meeting House Square. Tel: 670 5372

Definitely one of the 'in' places to be seen eating in Dublin, Eden carries with it an air of exclusivity. Catering for more expensive tastes, this can be a little off-putting to the budget traveller. But the food is excellent and the wine list extensive, while in the summer the view of the bustling square can be quite a treat.

Main course from £11 to £18

ELEPHANT & CASTLE

18 Temple Bar. Tel: 679 3121

There's an informal atmosphere here, together with some of the tastiest dishes in town, and a decent wine menu to boot. Specialising in omelettes and in hamburgers (the Elephant burger is just the thing if you're hungry), the Elephant & Castle also does a mean salad and the chicken wings are well worth a try. You'd better arrive early or you might have a lengthy wait of up to an hour, because they don't take bookings.

Main course from £5 to £15

ENVY
13 Crown Alley. Tel: 670 3161

Easily missed, but don't! An original menu and a wonderful atmosphere make Envy a great place to visit. This is definitely one of the cooler places to eat in Temple Bar, while the food is very impressive too. Just the place for a quiet bite.

Main course up to £9

FAN'S RESTAURANT
60 Dame Street. Tel: 679 4263

A Cantonese restaurant, Fan's is popular with Dubliners and tourists alike. The atmosphere is clean and sedate, erring on the side of quiet rather than boisterous. The food is all you could hope for, as is the service.

Main course from £8.50 to £11.50

FITZERS CAFÉ
Temple Bar Square. Tel: 679 0440

One of a chain of similarly titled restaurants in Dublin, Fitzers serves cuisine with a recognisable international bent, in a friendly atmosphere.

Main course from £8 to £14

FITZSIMONS

Essex Street East

Usually packed out on any sporting or rugby weekend, Fitzsimons attracts a mixed crowd, where trendier fashions rub shoulders with business suits. And to cap it all, you can also catch a good traditional session here, or even some set-dancing early in the week. Part of the Wellington Quay Hotel.

THE FOGGY DEW

Fownes Street

In the not too distant past, this was one of the dingiest bars in Temple Bar, much loved by the locals who could enjoy a good pint without being set upon by the younger elements of the city. That's all changed, and though some of the old clientèle will complain about the Dew's face-lift, there's no denying that it has much more to offer the traveller these days. Mosaics are the highlight of an impressive interior, and you can still get a good pint. Some of the locals continue to drink here, but a trendier crowd has claimed the bar for its generation.

LES FRÈRES JACQUES

74 Dame Street. Tel: 679 4555

Specialising, not surprisingly, in French cuisine, this restaurant has an enviable reputation for its fare. Situated beside the Olympia Theatre, it serves a variety of dishes but is best known for its seafood. Definitely one to try if your pocket can stretch to it. Enjoy the live piano music as you eat.

Main course up to £19

THE FRONT LOUNGE
Parliament Street

One of the most popular establishments in Temple Bar, the Front Lounge is largely responsible for a shift in focus of the area westwards towards Parliament Street. If the Foggy Dew and the Auld Dubliner were the centre of Temple Bar for a previous generation, Parliament Street is the choice of a new one. The Front Lounge lays claim to a young, fashionable atmosphere. The comfortable chairs and couches belie the less than relaxed mood of many of the patrons who are on a night out. A good bar for all that, it can come into its own earlier in the day, when a quiet pint can be heaven.

GALLAGHER'S BOXTY HOUSE
20 Temple Bar. Tel: 677 2762

The Boxty House is, not surprisingly, a hit with tourists, and though some of the locals view their native cuisine with more than a little suspicion, there's no questioning the restaurant's popularity. Traditional fare here includes boxty — an Irish potato cake, cooked on a griddle and filled with meat and vegetables; coddle — a stew of sausages, bacon and potatoes; Irish stew; and bacon and cabbage.

Main course from £6 to £13

Food and Drink

LA GONDOLA

Asdill's Row. Tel: 677 5758

An out-of-the-way Italian restaurant situated almost beside the Ha'penny Bridge, La Gondola serves good food at a competitive price. You can expect all of the usual pasta dishes.

Main course from £6 to £12

HANDEL'S

Fishamble Street

Attached to the George Frederic Handel Hotel, on one of Dublin's oldest streets, this bar and restaurant serves a variety of dishes priced very competitively.

Main course from £4 to £10

THE HA'PENNY INN

Wellington Quay

One of the few places near the heart of Temple Bar to hang on to its old clientèle, the Inn has succeeded admirably in attracting a younger crowd without destroying the old décor that keeps its regulars happy. A rare throwback to how pubs in Temple Bar used to look, the Inn is part of Dublin's burgeoning comedy scene, hosting a comedy night every week.

HEAVENLY FOOD COMPANY

Temple Bar Square

Although there's not much room to sit, the coffee here is definitely of the heavenly variety and sure to provide a good picker-upper for anybody caught by the cold blasts from the Liffey.

THE HOSTEL CAFÉ

See Oliver St John Gogarty's.

THE INTERNET CAFÉ

Temple Lane

Does exactly what you would expect, with rows of computers and monitors providing the backdrop for a cup of coffee. Mainly for those in need of an electronic fix.

IRISH FILM CENTRE

Eustace Street

Hardly surprisingly, this is one of Temple Bar's trendier spots to be seen in. It offers a wide selection of bar food, including a good vegetarian menu. Cool and with wide open spaces, the IFC can still become very packed and smoky later on, as people out for the evening rub shoulders with cinema-goers. Though the food is good, it's more of a place to start a night's entertainment in, rather than become the focus of the evening, and it's a particularly good spot for a group. A perfect place for a drawn-out conversation over a pint.

ISOLDE'S TOWER

Essex Street West

A bar, restaurant and club all rolled into one, Isolde's Tower is one of the favourite night spots in Temple Bar. Although older drinkers may find the atmosphere a little cramped and manic as the night goes on, younger patrons will love the non-stop music and party atmosphere. This hostelry is named after one of the city's defences which used to be situated on Essex Quay.

JASKO'S BISTRO

Dame Street. Tel: 679 7767

A relaxed, quiet atmosphere combined with real quality serves to put Jasko's right at the top of the restaurant league in Temple Bar, though you'd never guess it from the exterior of the building. Serving seafood as well as meat dishes, Jasko's also conjures up some good vegetarian choices, although you may have to ask for them specifically.

Main course from £8 to £14

THE JOY OF COFFEE

Essex Street East

If there's a better way of relaxing in Temple Bar, then I don't know it. The Joy of Coffee serves one of the best cuppas in the quarter as well as snacks. But the real joy isn't in the food or drink, it's in the relaxed atmosphere There's no chance of you being rushed over your solitary cup of coffee here, and there are plenty of free papers and guides to keep you going.

Food and Drink

THE LEFT BANK

Anglesea Street

One of the hipper spots to be seen in when around town, the Left Bank attracts a young and trendy crowd, but don't let that put you off. The bar is worth visiting, if only to see the old converted vault downstairs. The pints are rather good and they serve traditional Irish pub grub as well.

LITTLE SICILY

Parliament Street

Not difficult to figure out what they serve here. Definitely a spot for those travelling on a tight budget, Little Sicily will send you on your way with some good, honest Italian food. Main course from £5 to £8

LUCKY'S

Dame Street

A typical café offering coffee and snacks.

LUIGI MALONE'S

Cecilia Street. Tel: 670 2723

Whether you're after a mid-afternoon cocktail or a three-course meal, this Irish-Italian place can help you. The food is a mix of Italian and international — burgers and salads jostle with pizzas and pastas on the menu. Pitchers of beer can be ordered as readily as a bottle of wine to get the mood going. The interior is wide and bright, and for some reason there's a propeller hanging from the roof. A handy place for groups and families, but not the best location for a private meeting.

Main course from £6 to £14

LA MED
22 Essex Street East. Tel: 670 7358

Not surprisingly, as its name suggests, La Med serves food with a Southern European flavour, in a pleasant and cheerful environment. Though a little pricier than some of its neighbouring restaurants, it does offer a variety of dishes and wines.

Main course from £9 to £14

THE MERMAID CAFE
69/70 Dame Street. Tel: 670 8236

Serving what it describes as 'fine Irish ingredients' cooked in an 'east-coast style' the Mermaid is a popular restaurant situated on one of Dublin's busiest streets. The food is good, and the atmosphere is congenial to an enjoyable evening. The Mermaid has won several awards which are proudly displayed on its wall.

Main course from £12 to £17

MEXICO TO ROME
Temple Bar. Tel: 677 2727

Serves just what the name would suggest. Definitely one of the more cheerful restaurants in town, this establishment can be relied upon for a good night's entertainment at the right price.

Main course from £7 to £11

Food and Drink

LA MEZZA LUNA

1 Temple Lane. Tel: 671 2840

Though the front door is on Dame Street, you have to go around the corner to Temple Lane to get into La Mezza Luna, but the extra few yards are well worth the stroll. One of many Italian restaurants in the area, La Mezza Luna proves that you can have good food at a reasonable price. The Mediterranean atmosphere here complements the imaginative pastas well.

Main course from £7 to £15

MILANO'S

Temple Bar. Tel: 670 3384

More familiar to British tourists as the 'Pizza Express', Milano's has two restaurants in Dublin (the other is on Dawson Street). Both offer the same range of pizzas and pastas at very affordable prices, and in plusher surroundings than you might expect from a pizzeria. A handy spot for those who have arrived in Temple Bar hungry, but haven't thought to book ahead for a table.

Main course from £4 to £7

MONGOLIAN BARBEQUE

7 Anglesea Street. Tel: 670 4154

One of the most interesting eating experiences in Temple Bar, you'll definitely have to book ahead if you want to eat at this hugely popular restaurant. A hit with both locals and tourists, the Mongolian offers a fun atmosphere and all you eat for £11. Choose what you would like from a wide variety of meats, vegetables and spices, and then queue up to watch it stir-fried by chefs.

MONTY'S

28 Eustace Street. Tel: 670 4911

One of the more unusual discoveries of Temple Bar, Monty's specialises in Nepalese fare at very reasonable prices. Excellent food in relaxed surroundings. Quentin Tarantino ate here when in town and they have his signature to prove it.

Main course from £7 to £13

NICO'S

53 Dame Street. Tel: 677 3062

A great Italian, Nico's is among the most successful restaurants of Temple Bar, and definitely a spot favoured by the natives. You can expect the best of Italian food here, tasty if a little conservative, and the highlight of any night's eating has to be the piano music, which sets a very moody atmosphere for diners.

Main course from £8 to £13

THE NORSEMAN

Essex Street East

Along with the Temple Bar, and the Palace, this is one of the area's landmark bars. Although (like many local bars) it has undergone a major refurbishment in recent years, it hasn't lost too much of its original charm. You'll usually find the pub packed whatever time you arrive, as students, tourists and locals all compete with each other for service at the bar. Its name recalls the rich legacy of Viking Dublin.

THE OAK

Dame Street

More like part of Thomas Read's than a separate pub, the crowd that frequents the Oak is a little less trendy than that which inhabits the other half of the building. A considerably smaller and quieter bar than Read's, the Oak is a convenient place for a quieter drink or a handy place to go if you can't get near the bar in Read's.

THE OLD MILL

14 Temple Bar, Merchant's Arch. Tel: 671 9262

Offering, in its own words, 'good food at reasonable prices', the Old Mill can be a little hard to locate, its entrance almost hidden away between two shop fronts. Open all week long, it serves European fare with a French flavour.

Main course from £8 to £12

OLIVER GOLDSMITH'S

Dame Street

Part of the Trinity Arch Hotel, this bar is one of two named for a literary Oliver. Goldsmith's is much newer to Temple Bar than the other Oliver, but has proven a popular spot. Beautifully decorated inside, as is the hotel, it's a pleasant place to drink and relax, but it does get busy at the weekends.

OLIVER ST JOHN GOGARTY'S

Temple Bar

Vying with the Quays for the title of busiest bar, the Oliver St John (pronounced Sinjin) Gogarty is named for the writer, and the literary connection still remains as the renowned Literary Pub Crawl of Dublin has made this bar one of its top stops. The bar serves excellent pub grub and has regular traditional music sessions, designed to get the toes tapping. And the pints flowing. Another bar where movement is difficult on rugby weekends. The Hostel Café is owned by the bar's proprietors and serves a variety of reasonably priced traditional Irish food.

Food and Drink

O'SHEA'S

23 Anglesea Street. Tel: 671 9049

With a menu offering more traditional Irish food, O'Shea's has proven popular with many tourists on the lookout for something more substantial.

Main course from £7 to £11

THE PALACE BAR

Fleet Street

Still the most attractive bar in the area, the Palace Bar retains its original beautiful wood panelling and partitions, quirky stained-glass ceiling, and genial atmosphere. It is also well renowned for serving one of the best pints of stout to be had around this part of the city. A known haunt of local journalists, the pub also enjoys quite a lot of trade from visiting professors attending nearby Trinity College. If you're after atmosphere, a good pint and some peace and quiet, try this bar. Usually busy in the evenings.

THE PALM TREE

16 Temple Bar. Tel: 679 8238

Another of the newer restaurants to spring up in Temple Bar, The Palm Tree offers fresh, competitively priced dishes from seafood and Irish meat to crabtoes and freerange chickens. All desserts are homemade, like their delicious cappicino cheesecake.

Main course from £5 to £9

La Paloma

Asdill's Row. Tel: 677 7392

The Spanish may be outnumbered by the Italians in Temple Bar, but this restaurant does its best to redress the balance. Serving huge paellas as well as tortillas, and of course Spanish wine, La Paloma provides flamenco music (on tape, not live) for those seeking something a little different. With the brightly coloured walls, the atmosphere here is so Mediterranean you'd almost think you were in West Cork! Main courses from £7 to £12.

Planet Web

Essex Street East

Internet Café, serving good food.

Poco Loco

32 Parliament Street. Tel: 679 1950

A small, cute bistro offering Tex-Mex food at very affordable prices. You can enjoy the colourful surroundings as you order single or double portions without breaking the bank. Described by one restaurant guide as 'The Lego Approach to Mexican Food'.

Main course from £5 to £9

The Porterhouse Brewing Company

Parliament Street

The Porterhouse brews a wide range of its own beers and

stouts, all designed to leave you with varying degrees of fondness for the place. Some visitors will remember this micro-brewery for the lovely in-terior and the subtlety of some of the home-brewed stouts, while others will curse it the morning after, when they're still recovering from the effects of one or two of the stronger ales. Live music is a regular feature here, and there's food as well. But the most impressive features remain the huge vats in which the home-made stuff is brewed.

THE QUAYS BAR
Temple Bar Square

Another of the new bars to spring up in the quarter, the Quays is quite possibly the busiest bar in the area. Frequented by a mixture of the young and the trendy, the two-storey bar is decorated in traditional style but is geared for a modern clientèle. Serves good beer and there's also live music.

QUEEN OF TARTS
Lord Edward Street

A cute little café offering pâtisserie and coffee, the cheerfully titled Queen of Tarts provides a little respite from the climb to Christchurch Cathedral from the Olympia Theatre.

THE REFECTORY, KINLAY HOUSE
Lord Edward Street

Small café set in a student atmosphere, the Refectory offers cheap snacks and coffee for the budget traveller.

Food and Drink

THE SENATE

Lord Edward Street

Part of the Forum Hotel, the Senate is a good place to go for a drink when the rest of Temple Bar is thronged. Located opposite to City Hall, the Senate serves some bar food, but is primarily a handy spot for a quiet drink, whether you're a part of a couple or a group. There's also a hotel restaurant.

SHACK

Essex Street East and Lord Edward Street. Tel: 670 0043

The only business to have a chain of restaurants in Temple Bar (two!), the Shack is a popular venue for diners. Serving a variety of traditional Irish fare and European dishes, the restaurants have much more of an Irish feeling than many of their more cosmopolitan neighbours.

Main course from £8 to £13

SHIRAZ

Eustace Street

A new restaurant specialising in seafood and pastas, this Italian establishment is located beside Bruno's. Good food is complemented by a pleasant dining atmosphere, and both are helped

greatly by an extensive wine list.

Main course from £9 to £13

SINNERS

Parliament Street. Tel: 671 9345

Sinners has become a very popular dining spot in Dublin, almost as much for the regular appearances of its belly-dancers as for its food. The cuisine here is Lebanese, and though it is possible to enjoy a quiet tryst, the emphasis is on enjoying your meal. The subject of much press coverage since its opening, the restaurant regularly enjoys the patronage of Middle-Eastern politicians and dignitaries when they are in town.

Main course from £9 to £13

TANTE ZOË'S

1 Crow Street. Tel: 679 4407

One of the oldest restaurants in Temple Bar, this was also the first to offer genuine Cajun/Creole dishes. It's still one of the best, and its moody atmosphere is helped greatly by its location in dimly lit Crow Street. Whether you opt for chargrilled swordfish or Surf n' Turf steak, you won't be disappointed, while the wine list is excellent and caters for all wallet sizes.

Main course from £8 to £12

THE TEA ROOMS

The Clarence Hotel, 6-8 Wellington Quay. Tel: 670 7766

If the Clarence is one of the most stylish hotels in Dublin, the

Tea Rooms are the jewel in this particular crown. At once a superb restaurant and one of the hippest places in town, the Tea Rooms afford both the casual tourist and the determined local a chance to sample the hotel's delights. You'll be spoiled for choice with an impressive menu, but if you don't want to feel out of place, dress up a bit and don't stare at your fellow diners, no matter how famous they are.

Main course from £15 to £19

THE TEMPLE BAR
Essex Street East

One of the places to go in Dublin if you're after a bit of craic, the Temple Bar has a long and proud history of pulling pints for locals and generally giving punters a good night out. Though the décor won't win prizes, few patrons worry about such a minor matter. The emphasis is on enjoying yourself. On rugby weekends you can forget about getting a pint.

THE TEMPLE BAR CAFÉ
Temple Lane South

Somewhere to stop off for a snack as you traverse Dublin's cultural quarter.

THAI ORCHID
Fleet Street. Tel: 671 9969

Offering Thai dishes, this eatery on the corner of Fleet Street and Westmoreland Street guards the main eastern entrance to

Temple Bar. Providing a taste of the exotic, the Orchid gives diners a chance to try something a little out of the ordinary. Main course from £7 to £12

THOMAS READ'S
Parliament Street
Along with the Front Lounge, this is one of the most fashionable hang-outs for Dublin's young and trendy set. Occupying one of the best sites in town, it's located opposite City Hall and Dublin Castle, not far away from the Olympia Theatre. The selection of alcohol reflects the wealthy and varied clientèle, but if you fancy dropping in for curiosity's sake, don't feel self-conscious — just strike a pose and get down to it.

THUNDER ROAD CAFÉ
Temple Bar. Tel: 679 4057
Although the first of the burger/rock joints in Dublin, the Thunder Road Café is one of the most popular, and it's usually packed with young people intent on having a good time. Loud music and video screens accompany the waiters and waitresses who often lead the clientèle in table-top dancing sessions, while bouncers and Harley Davidsons keep watch outside. Main course around £7

TOPOLIS
Parliament Street. Tel: 670 4961
Another Italian, Topolis offers good value for money and, as

might be expected, specialises in pastas and pizzas.

Main course from £6 to £10

TRASTEVERE

Temple Bar Square. Tel: 670 8343

One of the more fashionable Italian restaurants to be seen in, Trastevere occupies an enviable location at Temple Bar Square. The usual pastas and pizzas are on offer, though the emphasis is on more inventive food than many other similarly priced restaurants. You will not be rushed here, but you will need to book a table as the restaurant is exceptionally popular.

Main course from £5 to £12

THE TURK'S HEAD CHOP HOUSE

Parliament Street

With possibly the most original name of all the city's pubs, the Turk's Head has developed something of a niche for itself in recent years. The interior of the bar matches the name, but the crowd is young and friendly and not too over the top. There's a nightclub downstairs for those who want to have a bit of a bop. Definitely worth a visit.

VILLAGE GREEN COFFEE DOCK

Dame Street

Another of the many cafés which dot Temple Bar, this one sits on the southern periphery, offering shoppers and tourists a brief respite from the bustling crowds outside.

THE WALL STREET CAFÉ

Crown Alley

One of the smaller establishments in the area, the Wall Street is well known to locals and to business people who work in the area. Food here is straightforward but honest.

THE WOOD QUAY BAR

Fishamble Street

A more upmarket bar than most, the Wood Quay draws a regular crowd from the council's nearby Civic Offices, as well as a number of locals. Though quiet during the day, it gets busier in the evenings and at weekends.

Bibliography

Bennett, Douglas, Encyclopaedia of Dublin.

Graby, John and Deirdre O'Connor, Dublin.

Healy, Elizabeth et al., The Book of the Liffey.

Liddy, Pat, Temple Bar – Dublin. An illustrated History.

McLoughlin, Adrian, Guide to Historic Dublin.

O'Dwyer, Frederick, Lost Dublin.

THE WOLFHOUND GUIDE TO HURLING

Brendan Fullam

Hurling is arguably the oldest field game in the world in which strength, speed, stamina, skill, and endurance are the key qualities. Over the centuries it has evolved into a more regulated but still exciting and passionate game.

In this *Guide to Hurling* Brendan Fullam investigates the origins and evolution of this much-loved game.

He discusses its requirements and its attractions, the competitions and grades, the GAA founders and the great players.

A treasure for anyone who wants to know more about this quintessentially Irish game.

ISBN 0-86327-724-1

THE WOLFHOUND GUIDE TO
THE SHAMROCK
Bob Curran

No other plant is as intertwined with both the
history and folklore of Ireland as the shamrock. It
has become the very symbol of Ireland and of
Irishness world-wide. Like Ireland and her children,
it has been extolled in song, story and poem.

In this fascinating book, Bob Curran explores the
traditions of the shamrock, from its pre-Christian
beginnings through its pivotal rôle in the story
of Ireland's patron saint, Patrick, to its association
with Irish politics.

**A must for Irish and lovers of the Irish
everywhere!**

ISBN 0-86327-726-8